Being Seyboro

"Diesel" Dave Galloway

Tom Bradshaw (1952-2019)

Tom Bradshaw was born in 1952 in Roanoke, Virginia. He grew up in Roanoke, graduated from the high school there, and was accepted into the Army's WestPoint Academy. After graduating from WestPoint, he proudly served in the U.S. Army for four years. Tom then went on to make his living in the medical administration field and retired as the vice president of hospital operations at Wayne Memorial Hospital in Goldsboro, NC.

Tom was a lifelong cyclist, and I met him shortly after he moved to Goldsboro in the year 2000. He and I spent many of our days riding together, and the most memorable ones are the annual 5-day bike Virginia events. We would spend our days on the bikes, and our evenings sitting around a table, sharing a few beers, and swapping stories about the day's ride, and other memorable cycling adventures we had shared. It was always worth the while to recall those memories.

Tom was a kind, soft-spoken man who dearly loved his family, friends, and co-workers. Unfortunately, he was taken from this life far too early, as a victim of ALS, or Lou Gehrig's disease, in 2019. It was just a few years since he had retired and was looking forward to a relaxed life with his wife, Barbara, his children, grandson, and many of his friends and family, but fate had some other plans for him in the heavens above.

Joe Austin (1966-2019)

Joe Austin was born in 1965 in Minot, North Dakota. He was the son of a military man. He joined the Air Force himself and moved many times during his career. He ended up in Goldsboro, where he retired and began working in the same hospital as Tom Bradshaw. Joe, his wife Pat, and both of their daughters were all active cyclists, and we warmly welcomed them into our Seyboro family. Joe loved to ride, and I never saw him turn down an opportunity to get out for some miles. Cycling was not all winning for him. He genuinely had an attachment to this sport. He was often the one on our group rides to drop back and pick up a rider who was struggling to keep up the pace.

Joe traveled with our group on several occasions when we rode the Great Allegany Passage and C&O Canal, which run from Pittsburg, PA, through Cumberland, MD, and into Washington, D.C. He was in his element on these multi-day rides; we never saw him without a smile on his face. He was always the first to begin loading and unloading all the equipment that we carried with us. He would politely tell me, *"Get out of the way, Old Man! Let me get that for you."*

He was famous for his normal greeting of *"Hey, Brother!"* and he truly was a brother to all of us. He never stayed back from helping any of us. He had a kind heart and a generous soul. Joe passed away unexpectedly in his sleep in the spring of 2019 and was taken from us at the young age of 54. We miss him like anything, especially on the windy days we often think of Joe. He's the one who would get up in the front of the pace line, and power us down the road.

Karl Gerschutz (1957-2013)

I first met Karl Gerschutz during the Gulf war when I was deployed in Oman. Karl approached me in the legal tent and said that he had seen me riding my bicycle around the camp. It turned out Karl had been riding a bike himself for a considerable time, and he was interested in joining a group. Because of our common love for cycling, we struck up an immediate friendship, and I told him about our club of Seyboros. *"When we get back home, you need to start riding with us,"* I told him. He became a regular visitor with me, asking lots of questions about riding and our club. My friend, Dave Scarano, who also had a bike in the desert, started visiting with us too, and we all dreamed of the day we would get back home to the U.S.A. and could begin riding with the Seyboro Cyclists again. That day finally came in March of 1991.

Karl was tall and lean, and it was evident from the beginning that he was a strong cyclist. He just needed to learn the nuances of riding with a group, and he caught on quickly. His first race took place in a Kinston ride in June of 1991. I broke away from the lead group at 50 miles, and the only one who could go with me was Karl. He hung onto my wheel, desperately for the last 15 miles. I kept saying, *"Come on, Karl, just hold my wheel,"* and he did. I finished first, followed by Karl in second place, and that's the last time I ever beat that rascal.

Karl rode with us for about 20 years. He retired from the Air Force and settled in Arizona. He still came to visit on certain occasions and always brought his bike with him. On

June 29, 2013, I received a fateful phone call from my friend Frank. Karl had crashed descending Mt Lemmon, near Tucson, Arizona, on a club ride. He was by himself at the time, no doubt leading the group, and several witnesses saw him go off the left side of the road in a sharp curve. He died instantly at the young age of 56. It was very unusual because Karl was such an experienced cyclist.

Three true friends, fellow Seyboro Cyclists are now apart with tons of memories to cherish. Thousands of miles spent together on the saddles of our bikes, yet not enough to fill the empty space in my heart ever since they left this world. My Christian faith assures me I will ride with them again in the next life, but I miss them, nonetheless. Each of these men was special in their own way, and any of them would have done anything in this world for me. I dedicate this book to their memories and hope I do them proud.

Acknowledgment

This book is a compilation of many years of fun and excitement in the Seyboro Cyclists Bicycle Club. Each and every member of the club has been a part of our history. I cannot remember a single time I finished a ride without having had a belly full of laughs and smiles along the way. It has only been possible because of our club and the unique personalities of all its members.

I do owe special thanks to some of our members, who helped me recall many of the names and dates of our club's history. Steve Desrochers, Frank Drohan, Mike Haney, Benny Hood, Ralph and Judy Jodice, Chuck Millard, Rick Sessions, Scott Summers, and Jörg Wagner – all these folks helped bring some of the names and stories to light. Jörg, Scott and Lisa Mathias helped in digging up some of the older photos. Also, I bounced a lot of thoughts and ideas off Jörg on our daily bike rides. I owe a huge thanks to all these folks who helped me get my thoughts onto paper.

I also need to acknowledge my Lord, Jesus, who has given me some extra years of life to fulfill my dream of writing my books. I have been to the death's doorsteps twice on separate occasions in the past, and my Lord kept me alive. I am incredibly grateful for the extra time He has given me!

About the Author

Diesel Dave Galloway is an aspiring author who recently released his 1st book, *'Making Seyboro.'* He continues his story in *'Being Seyboro'* about a bicycle club that he helped to co-find many years ago. The club has always been made up of a rare mixture of personalities that all come together and make life on two wheels exciting, challenging, and fun.

Those who know Dave can tell you he loves life on two wheels, be it a bicycle or a motorcycle. In 2004, his bicycle club recognized him for reaching a milestone. He had completed 100,000 miles on his bicycle ever since he started riding in 1984. He has traveled the country on a motorcycle as well and earned his 'Iron Butt' certificate when he and his brother, Mike, rode 1,000 miles in 24 hours in the N.C Tar Butt Motorcycle Rally.

Dave credits his family, large group of friends, and his Christian faith for the wonderful life he has enjoyed.

A SEYBORO MEMORY

On the Cover

In October of 2006, the Seyboros scheduled an 85-mile ride to Surf City, NC. We had about 30 cyclists and several SAG vehicles. On this Saturday, my wife Kay had offered to drive SAG, and she had my two little grandsons, Gabe and Caleb, with her. Gabe had just turned 5 and Caleb would soon be 3 years old, and they were the light of my life. These little guys were so proud and excited about PapPap and all the other adults riding their bikes.

Kay was driving the car with my little buddies sitting high in their car seats. She would drive ahead, park on the side of the road, and wait for us to come by. Each time we were greeted with cheers and clapping. We had planned a stop at a store about 25 miles from the finish, and Kay had agreed to meet us there with drinks and fruits. When we stopped, Kay pulled me aside and whispered, *"Dave, your grandsons think you are in a bike race, and they keep saying they sure hope their PapPap wins this race! They have said it about a dozen times now!"* Well, it wasn't really a race, but I didn't want to disappoint them. I knew when we got close to the finish there would be a sprint to see who could get there first.

We got back on the road, and I spoke with our strong riders. I asked, *"Hey guys, my grandkids think we are racing, and they really want their PapPap to win. Would you mind, just this time, letting me slip ahead of you, so I can throw my hands in the air and win this 'race', as they're calling it?"*

Of course, they all agreed, and when we made our last turn onto the road to the Surf City Welcome Center, they said, *"Go ahead, Dave, make your move."* I rode up ahead of them a little, and as we approached the Welcome Center, I saw my car with Kay standing there, cheering for me. As I rode toward them, I threw my hands in the air, just like they do in the Tour de France. However, as I was looking, I saw no sign of the boys.

When I got stopped, I asked Kay, *"Hey, where are Gabe and Caleb?"* She replied, *"We waited for a few minutes. And then they found a swing set out behind the building. They're back there playing on the swings."*

I had *'won'* the race, just for my Grandsons, and they weren't even there to see it. In effect, I had finished the race in second place, nipped at the line by a swing set!

Preface

The Seyboro Cyclists have been riding the roads of Goldsboro and Wayne County for thirty-five years now. Our claim to fame is that we have no rules, no official leaders, no formal structure. Just show up and ride with us, and you can consider yourself a Seyboro. There are Seyboros around the world now, as many of the club's members have moved on to new locations or new jobs. When these folks leave, they often come back to visit or keep in touch with the club members, and the common thread they relay to the club is *"There isn't another club in the world that shows the love and affection, or has the fun and excitement that the Seyboros share!"*

For many years I've dreamt of memorializing our club's history, and I'm excited to finally fulfil my dream. I'll take you from our very roots, and travel with you around North Carolina and to several different states as we rode together on our bikes, laughed and carried-on off the bikes, and just had a fantastic time spending time with each other. From the Natchez Trace in Mississippi, to the Hotter than Hell Hundred in Texas, the challenging mountains of North

Carolina and Virginia, and the various club "Tour de Fools" we rode, I hope to keep you entertained with our antics and pranks we played on one another, the many adventures we encountered, and mostly, the love and camaraderie we shared with one another. As we were always fond of saying to new members and visitors, "Follow Us!"

Contents

Page Left Blank Intentionally

Chapter 1
Father's Day, 1990

It was a warm Sunday morning in eastern North Carolina, a beautiful state of landscapes, and on top of that, it was the spring season of 1990. The flowers were blossoming, and it was a beautiful sight to witness as far as your eyes could see. It was a Father's Day, but not any other ordinary Father's Day. It was not going to be a typical Father's Day in North Carolina, where little kids made cards for their fathers, while adults posted pictures with them on social media networks. It was going to be a fulfilled day with many ups and downs.

The Seyboro club had arranged a day full of fun, not only for the fathers but for the mothers as well. The air was filled with discussions about what the day ahead was going to be like. A huge number of cyclists were descending on the small town of Mount Olive because that's where the Seyboro Cyclists' annual Father's Day ride was about to take place. There was a weird enthusiasm that could be felt in the air. Everyone was quite excited about the ride.

The fathers in the group of cyclists always like to joke that it was one of the few days during the year when they could ride without their spouses fussing at them to get some household chores done instead of riding their bikes. At least for one day, we were not told that the grass needed to be cut and weeds needed to be removed from the gardens. At least for one day, we were free spirits. On Father's Day, we would ride guilt-free; the chores could wait.

Well, today's ride is no ordinary ride. It would be a metric century, meaning 100 kilometers, or 62 miles. It was a long day ahead of us, but we were all determined. The word had spread throughout the area, as we were advertising a couple of SAG vehicles that would be available on the route for emergencies or bike malfunctions, you never know. Nevertheless, one certain thing was that nothing could stop us from riding that day. We also had a water and food stand at about the 35-mile point of the ride so that if any of us felt the need to stop and restore energy, we could do so without having anything to lose. Not only men but also women of all ages showed up decked in their colorful cycling gear, many riding bicycles worth several thousands of dollars. Cycling is that one thing that unites everyone at one platform, while also being fun, good for the environment, and good for the body. It is one of those rare sports that are healthy, also considered as a low-impact exercise that can be enjoyed by people of all ages, from young children to older adults. There was an excited, friendly crowd of cyclists gathered in the Walmart parking lot where the ride would begin and end. Many of our family members were there as well to see us off and wish us a safe ride. Though cycling has many health benefits, most of us gathered for the fun element. The air was loaded with excitement, and none of us could wait for it to begin.

The Seyboro club was in its heyday back then, and it was not unusual for us to draw 100 or more riders for our events. People knew about us and recognized us as one of the best cycling institutions. People from all over eastern North Carolina were always ready to take part in our events, and there were about 100 participants present for this ride. As usual, we also drew a few friends from area bike clubs, of course, we had to make it fun for ourselves as well, and without the competition, it would become boring. The other bike clubs' primary mission was to try and be the first ones across the finish line and rub some Seyboro noses in the dirt, but that was not happening since we were all determined not to let that happen.

Not a Race, Yet a Race!

I know you must be wondering why I am not calling it a race already, because it was NOT. Our events were never advertised as a race. They were intended to be fun rides, a chance for cyclists to get together for a ride, enjoy each other's company, and bask in the beautiful weather. Though the weather is not always beautiful, only true cyclists would know the joy of riding with a huge number of people. It gives you a sense of belongingness, a sense of mission that we need to accomplish together.

Although our intention is never to turn it into a race, any competitive cyclist can tell you that anytime you get two or more cyclists together, there will definitely be a competitive edge to the ride, regardless of the gender. There is always some silent chest-thumping going on, and several questions arise in our heads. We look at the other riders and try to gauge their abilities. Are their legs shaved? How about their quads and calves? What brand of bike are they riding? Shimano or Campy components? Have they ridden as many miles as I have? We never admit it out loud, but most of us are thinking about these things in our heads. Don't get me wrong because many participants are genuinely just out to have a fun ride. Nonetheless, there will always be a silent competition going on between some of the riders that you would have no idea about.

"Winning isn't everything; it's the only thing."

-Vince Lombardi

We competitive Seyboros had a primary mission to make sure that one of us finished the ride before anyone else. It was unfathomable to think of being the sponsor of the ride, and letting some 'outsider' finish first, and get all the glory. At least for us competitive Seyboros, it would be a disgrace, and we could not digest it.

So, there were about a dozen of the competitive riders among our group of Seyboros that followed this primary mission, and I was one of them. We would work together as a team for about 61 ½ miles, and then it was every man for himself as we battled it out for the finishing line. We planned on finishing non-stop in about 2 hours and forty minutes with our tongues hanging out, barely able to breathe, thirsty, covered in sweat, and road grime. None of us cared about anything, except for finishing what we started.

"When your legs scream to stop, and your lungs are bursting, that's when it starts. That's the hurt locker. Winners love it in there."

-Chris McCormack

The other riders would probably have a lot more fun than us because they were not focused on finishing first. They would ride at a reasonable pace, enjoy the beautiful scenery, stop for water or sodas and snacks in between, and chat along the way. Most would finish an hour or even more behind us, but they will get the same trophy as the first-place finisher, meaning, none!

Preparing for the ride

As we prepared to start the ride, one of our strongest riders, Frank Drohan, came around to all of the club members and told us that his wife, Linda, was going to be driving SAG, meaning she would be accompanying us on the route in her Chevy Suburban. *"Give your extra water bottles to Linda,"* Frank said. *"She's gonna be with us the entire ride."*

It's worth mentioning that most road bikes are equipped with one or two water bottle cages because riding a bicycle means you are going to need water every mile or two. A full water bottle weighs a pound or more, and we being the avid cyclists, pay a lot of money for a bike that weighs 20 pounds or less. We try to make the bike as light as possible, so why add extra weight when we don't have to?

What we do is we give our extra bottles to the SAG driver and have them hand us bottles out of the car window on the fly when we need them. Carrying as little extra weight a possible is one way of making the ride easier for us. It also may make the difference in a sprint for the finish line in a sport that is often won by inches.

Most of us carried four to five water bottles since it was warm outside, and we would be working hard. We needed that much fluid to get us through the ride. Therefore, we decided that instead of carrying all that weight, we should give all our bottles to Linda. We carried one bottle each, and Linda would hand us an extra bottle out of the car's window when we needed one. This was our plan.

Finally, the ride begins!

The ride started at 9 a.m., and all of us headed east on Highway 55. The route was not so simple but easy to understand. We would be riding a large rectangle, taking us close to the towns of Goldsboro and Smithfield, but most of the roads would be rural with little traffic. As soon as the ride began, all of us were pushing ourselves to the limit. I am talking about the competitive Seyboros here since we were focusing on our primary mission; to finish the race first.

About ten minutes into the ride, I heard someone calling my name. I turned around to find it was my friend Dave Scarano. He said to me, *"Hey, Dave! Take a look at Frank and tell me if you notice anything strange."* I immediately looked up ahead; Frank was leading the group at the time. I noticed he had two bottles of water on his bike, and another bottle of water in each of his three back jersey pockets. He looked like a camel. I sprinted up beside him and asked, *"Frank, how come you didn't give your extra bottles to Linda?"* He chuckled and replied, *"Dave, you should know by now, Linda can't read a map!"* *"What about our bottles?"* I asked. *"You guys are on your own,"* he laughed.

Needless to say, we never saw Linda. We had been conned by Frank, though not the first time, and unfortunately not for the last either. At that time, Frank was probably the fastest in our club. He was also one of the oldest. He took his riding very seriously and would take any advantage he could to finish first. We realized he was having fun at our expense, and none of us were surprised or angry. We would obviously find water somewhere. We also knew that if we stopped to fill our water bottles, Frank would keep riding, not losing any opportunity to get ahead of us, and we would have to chase him down each time.

Within a few miles into the ride, the front pack had been established. It included Frank, Brian Brothers, Rick Sessions, Dave Scarano, Tim Scott, Paul Harrell, Mike Luke, Eric Barnes, Larry Vaniwarden, me, and several other Seyboros. It also included about half a dozen riders from other bike clubs. We powered along at about 23-24 miles per hour, taking turns up the front of the pack, dropping back when we started to tire. Our water bottles were now empty, and we could not take the thirst anymore. Therefore, most of us stopped in the town of LaGrange to quickly refill our bottles, while Frank rode on, but we were not giving up easily. We hammered down the road and caught him about 3 miles later. We soon realized that this cycle was going to repeat itself several times that day.

Hell's Angels on bicycles?

There was one water stop that stands out in my mind. I laugh and feel bad at the same time when thinking about it. We were about thirty miles into the ride, and everybody except Frank had rerun out of water. We were on the Old Smithfield Highway at that time, hoping to come across a country store that would be open on a Sunday morning.

Fortunately, as we were passing a house on the right side of the road, suddenly our eyes met a lady who was watering her garden with a water hose. Someone among us shouted, *"Water on the right!"* Hearing this, we all slowed down, and the entire group, except for Frank, of course, pulled up into the lady's yard. She took one look at us - a look of horror in her eyes - then dropped the water hose and ran for her house. We started yelling at her that we just needed water, but she obviously didn't hear us or was not going to believe us. She must be wondering if we were hell's angels on bicycles, we may have looked that way to her. We felt kind of bad that we had scared her, but that was not our intention at all. At the same time, it didn't stop us from using her hose to fill our bottles, either. We were quickly back on the road with our bottles filled, again on the mission of chasing Frank and leaving one traumatized lady in our wake.

Slowly, we reeled Frank back in. Our group now numbered about eight riders; we had dropped the others behind. We powered on, riding as hard as we could. Each of us was beginning to dream of victory. With about five miles remaining, we started up a short but steep hill. As soon as we reached the hill, Frank lowered his head and powered away from the rest of us. Dave Scarano had enough left in his legs to chase after him, but the rest of us were done. Dave caught up with Frank, and we watched the two of them slowly open a gap on us. We realized we didn't have the energy to catch them, so we eased up a little. *"Nothing wrong with third place,"* each of us was thinking.

Who finished it first?

It didn't come as a surprise for any of us as Frank went on to finish first. Later we found out that Dave Scarano again fell victim to Frank's wily ways as well. About a mile from the finish line, Frank and Dave were still together. Frank said, *"See this house up ahead on the right?"* Dave replied, *"Yeah."* Frank went on to tell Dave there is a 'cat lady' living in the house. *"What's a cat lady?"* Dave asked. *"It's this lady who owns hundreds of cats. They're everywhere. If you slow down just a little and look closely, you're gonna see more cats in one place than you can imagine."* Frank was in front at the time, and Dave slowed down, looking to his right for cats. He didn't see any. *"Where are the cats?"* he asked.

After a few seconds of getting no reply, Dave looked up to ask again and noticed Frank had opened up a gap of about 10 yards and was sprinting just as fast as he could. Dave came out of his saddle and gave chase, but the damage was done. Frank had gained the physical and psychological advantage with his story about the cat lady, and there was no catching him now!

Hence, this was the ending of a typical fun and exciting Seyboro ride, just one of many. To this day, before we start a ride, somebody jokes around saying, *"Hey, are we gonna give our extra bottles to Linda?!!"*

Chapter 2
Six Years Earlier

At this point, when I look back at my life, I feel blessed to see how far I have come. I feel happy and proud that I have been able to reach a point in life where I am content with everything I am surrounded with; a beautiful family, loving wife, and my passion for cycling. It wasn't an easy journey, but it sure was worth it, and I can proudly say today that I did not just exist, I lived.

I have always been very ambitious and full of life, and when I say ambitious, I mean a whole lot of things. Before we dive into that, though, let's have some glimpses from my past. When I was younger, I used to think that there was nothing on this planet that I couldn't do. I have always been very lively, and people have always seemed to enjoy my company. I love trying new things, but not necessarily good things, and due to this one attribute, I got into smoking at the age of twenty-two.

Smoke or Suffer!

It was my third day in the Air Force, and as part of our basic training, we were required to spend long periods of time standing at attention. I listened to many of my fellow Airmen complaining about how badly they wanted a cigarette. I felt glad that I didn't smoke, but on the third day of basic training, our drill instructor said, *"Light 'em up if you got 'em."* Well, half of the guys lit up their cigarettes and started talking with one another. We, the non-smokers, were required to remain standing rigidly at attention, looking straight ahead. It did not seem fair; it was like we were being punished for not smoking. The next time the instructor said 'light 'em up,' I turned to the guy next to me and asked for a cigarette. I did not know at that time that this cigarette was not going to leave my side for a while now. I was hooked for the next ten years.

Quitting Smoke and Aftereffects!

I tried not once but many times to quit smoking, and finally, my daughter, Missy, who was seven at the time, made me a deal. Well, if you have read my previous book, you should be aware of my history in the Air Force and my sweet little family. The deal that Missy presented was that if I quit smoking, she'd do away with her security blanket. So, we made the deal, and I quit. I believe it's safe to say that I am among those rare humans who quit smoking for good.

It was 1984, and quitting smoking started to make me gain weight. I later learned the reason for weight gain was because nicotine increases the number of calories your body uses at rest by about 7% to 15%. Without cigarettes, your body may burn food more slowly. Cigarettes reduce appetite, so when you quit smoking, you may feel hungrier, and as a result, you gain weight. I had gained quite a few pounds, and whenever I looked at myself in the mirror, I could not believe what I had become. I became desperate to find effective ways to lose weight.

I was living a lazy lifestyle. Despite being in the Air Force at the time, I was still overweight. Since the Air Force is different from the Army and Marine Corps, we did not get up at five o'clock in the morning, and go on a 10-mile hike or run five miles nonstop. The Air Force's idea of physical fitness back then was that they would make you run a mile and a half, and you had to do it in a certain amount of time. Anybody who was in any kind of physical shape was normally able to run a mile and a half within the time provided by our regulations. Aside from the mile-and-a-half that I ran once a year, I was not into any other physical fitness activities. Due to my weight gain, I had started running daily but quickly discovered that running just wasn't for me.

How I Discovered Cycling All Over Again!

One day, I was sitting in my living room, surfing through channels. It was a warm afternoon in 1984 summer, and the best time to be at home. I was looking for something interesting to watch. I had my usual snacks with me, including a cold beer and a bag of chips. Suddenly, I came across a bicycle race and quickly realized I was watching the 1984 Olympic bicycle race happening in Los Angeles. I was never interested in cycling, although I had grown up riding a bike. This time, though, I was immediately captivated. The more I watched the race, the more intrigued I became.

This was a 120-mile bike race that took in several laps around the Los Angeles area, including climbing and descending some pretty impressive mountains. At the time, the group consisted of the top amateur cyclists from around the world. Since that time, the Olympic committee opened the race up to professionals, which I don't agree with. However, there were some impressive riders in the group, averaging around 27 to 28 miles per hour, if my memory serves me right. I listened while the commentators gave a lot of interesting insights and information about cycling, and explained a lot of strategies that the cyclists use. They explained how each country's riders would work together as a team to try and put their team members on the podium. The race was eventually won by Alexi Grewal, who was riding for the United States, which of course, made me proud, though I had never heard of this guy. He was the first and only American ever to win the Olympic road race.

To this day, I don't know what it was about watching this event on TV that got me so interested in cycling. I'd ridden a lot as a child and teenager, but the idea of a bunch of grown men riding around on bikes was totally foreign to me. Even though the race looked exciting, I distinctly remember thinking, *'it really doesn't look that hard.'* I believe the riders averaged maybe 26mph or a little more, but heck, 26mph didn't seem so fast in my car. I could do that!

Those Olympic guys had made riding a bike look so easy that as soon as the race was over, I went out back to my storage shed. I dug out my Schwinn LeTour bike that I'd bought from a friend and had never ridden. The tires were flat. A bunch of spiders had taken up residence. It took me about 30 minutes to get it decent enough to ride. After dusting it off, clearing the cobwebs, and pumping up the tires, I headed out for my first ride in many years.

How far could I ride? I was living on base and was intimately familiar with all the roads since I worked as a security policeman. I figured the furthest place on base from my house was the firing range. So, I headed out towards the range, not knowing how far I'd be riding. Surprisingly, it was pretty easy going. Actually, it was too easy!

Now I was on my old LeTour, heading to the firing range. I felt like I was doing at least 25mph if not faster. Heck, I didn't have a speedometer. I began thinking, *it isn't that tough. I could be in the Olympics.* I already imagined myself on television, racing my bike for the USA. Or maybe I'll be racing in the Tour de France, trying to avoid the paparazzi, signing autographs, avoiding my fans when I go out to eat. Why had it taken 33 years of my life to discover my talents?

Surprise! Surprise!

I finally made it to the firing range where the paved road ended and turned around to head home. But a funny thing happened when I arrived at the firing range. It took me about 15 minutes to get there from my house. When I turned around to head home, I immediately realized I was in big trouble. A strong headwind hit me flat in the face. I had never given the wind a thought. My Olympic aspirations started to plunge.

I'd been riding with a strong tailwind all the way to the range. So, my bubble was quickly burst, and it seemed like it took me several hours to get home. I have no idea how long it took me to get home, but I was crushed by the time I got there! (In reality, it was about 30 minutes). I suddenly had a newfound respect for the Olympians. What I mean to tell you is that I was hurting! I put the bike in the shed and limped into the house.

I had been living a rather sedentary lifestyle, and my lungs were suffering due to ten years of smoking cigarettes, sometimes two packs a day. My entire body was hurting. At the same time, something inside of me made me want to try riding again. I had caught the spirit. There was something about riding the bike that felt really good. I'd been riding a motorcycle since I was seventeen, and it was the same feeling of freedom, except the bicycle required a lot more work. The wind, the air, the openness, the smells, all those things you don't get in a closed vehicle.

My initial ride was under my belt, and I'd already learned a lesson; check the winds in advance. We always had some winds in eastern North Carolina, so I could not let it stop me from riding. Instead, I paid attention to the wind direction and was aware that sooner or later, I had to fight it. I went out the next day, riding the same route, this time paying some attention to the wind. I again realized that the wind could make a tremendous difference.

It was 1984, and many of today's cycling technologies didn't exist. Bicycle computers were just becoming available, but I didn't have one. The first thing I wanted to do was find out how far I had ridden. I got in my car and drove to the firing range and back. The round-trip distance was 6 ½ miles. OK, figuring my speed on a calculator revealed I'd averaged about 9mph. Maybe my Olympic aspirations were going to take a little longer than I'd thought, but that did not deter me. I liked this cycling stuff and decided to give it a try.

There was no going back!

I started riding the route once a day. I'd start my watch's timer and see how long it took me. I set a goal to ride a little bit faster each day and started making progress. Within a few weeks, I was riding the distance in 30 minutes. Now I was riding half as fast as the Olympians, but while they did it for 120 miles, I was only riding 6 ½ miles. I had my work cut out for me.

Persistence and dedication were the keys. I was stuck with it and found myself getting an emotional high each time I rode. My friend Frank would later tell me that the world would be a much better place if we could get the youngsters interested in competitive cycling at an early age. They wouldn't need drugs or alcohol to get high; the bike riding would provide the same effect.

Riding had become a daily experience for me; rain, shine, wind, or cold, I persisted. I learned some lessons along the way. One day, as I was turning around at the range, the bike started feeling funny; I looked down and realized I had a flat tire. This was before the cell phone days, and the firing range was on a remote side of the base. I ended up walking three miles to get home - I realized it was time to invest in a frame pump and a small saddle bag with a spare tube.

The days turned into weeks and weeks into months. I was definitely enjoying my rides, feeling stronger, and my timing was improving. I continued to get more efficient on the bike. I finally set a goal to try and average 20 mph on my rides, so I calculated I would have to complete the route in about 19 ½ minutes. It took me about three months, and I'll never forget the day I reached my goal. I was euphoric! I was thirsty to get better and faster, so I set a new goal of riding the route two times, or 13 miles a day.

'Every 'real' cyclist needs a 'racing' bike!

By now, I had started subscribing to cycling magazines, and studying the sport as much as I could. I was riding almost every day, only interrupted by heavy rain or family matters. I was rather proud of myself when I started keeping a mileage log and watched the miles add up. I soon determined I needed a better bike. At the time, a top-quality racing bike would cost $3,000 or better. I was enlisted in the Air Force, an E5 at the time, with a wife and three kids. We were living just barely above the poverty line. The first thing I needed to do was to convince Kay that I needed to buy a real racing bike. While $3,000 was out of my range, I found a Trek 520 bike at a bike shop in Kinston, NC. It sold for $500, which was a mountain of money to us at the time.

I started working on Kay, who was adamant that we couldn't afford it. Being the smart guy that I am, I knew if I kept bugging her, she would eventually give in. I even told her I would sell my motorcycle, and never ride one again (a fib that I had no intention of keeping). I kept insisting I needed that new bike, and one day, she succumbed by saying, *"Oh yeah, you just go ahead and buy that stupid bike and see what happens."* So, I did. I mean, she had permitted me, right?

I drove to Kinston and came home with the new Trek bike. I quickly realized that Kay had really meant, *"Don't you dare buy that bike."* After sleeping on the couch for a few nights, we made up, and she slowly began to accept my new obsession. Maybe I'll one day write a book on how to interpret what our wives actually mean by what they say.

As my timings of riding a bicycle improved with each passing day, I began thinking about trying to average 20 mph for my longer, 13-mile loop. After all, my goal was to improve as much as I could. Through all the research and everything I had studied related to cycling, I learned that serious cyclists riding in groups and participating in local races would normally maintain a speed of 20+ mph.

By now, I had got to the point where I was riding two loops, 13 miles, in 45 minutes, which meant I would need to trim about 5 minutes off my time. Not an easy task! I pushed myself to my limits. It wasn't easy, and it sure didn't happen overnight. Probably about seven or eight months into my cycling regimen, I did it; rode 13 miles, averaging 20 mph. I was ecstatic, and this encouraged me to work even harder!

My First Bike Race

Since I had now been riding for a while, my neighbors on both sides of me were taking notice of my exploits. My neighbor, Clarence, who was a big and powerful man, had taken note and started asking me some questions *like why was I doing it, how hard was it, how could I stand that narrow seat*, and so on. It turns out Clarence owned an old Sears 10-speed bike, so he dug it out of his shed and took a few rides.

Now Clarence was a mountain of a man, and the bike he owned was a rather small frame, so he looked somewhat comical riding on it. Nevertheless, I was glad to have influenced somebody else to ride. He didn't ride far, but I think he imagined the same things I did the first time I'd ridden; he would someday be participating in the Olympics.

One day, Clarence challenged me to a race. *"Oh, wow, my first bike race!"* I had seen him riding a few times, and don't think he'd ever done more than two or three miles, so I agreed. We would leave our homes, ride to the firing range and back two times, making 13 miles in total. Clarence had been watching me for months and insisted on a handicap. He would get a 10-minute head start. He was a little bit concerned that I would cheat and leave a few minutes earlier, so Kay agreed to be the official timekeeper. Yeah, he trusted her, but not me!

The big day came, Clarence headed out on his bike. Kay watched the timer like a hawk and gave me no slack. Anyway, Clarence took off to the cheers of thousands of fans (we can dream, can't we?). Ten minutes after he started, Kay gave me the go. I think she was rooting for Clarence because, by this time, I was obsessed with this cycling stuff, and she was probably tired of hearing about it. She was hoping I would get my wings clipped if I lost. I powered off and set my mind to the mission. When I was within a tenth of a mile from the turn-around on the first lap, I passed Clarence going the other way. He had that 'Oh crap' look on his face, *"Oh my golly,"* I thought. *"He's only got about a 2-minute lead on me."* This spurred me on even more, and about 2 miles from the finish of our first loop, I pulled up beside Clarence and patted him on the back. His startled look was worth a million dollars!

As I passed, I hollered, *"Don't give up, Clarence."* He uttered a few profanities at me. I finished the first lap a little later. The crowd had grown to several thousand people by now, or perhaps it was just Kay and my kids? Clarence came in about 5 minutes later; the race was over after just one lap. He was a little bit chagrinned, but still, a graceful loser. We drank a beer and discussed the fact that I had won my first bike race. Clarence was crushed but got over it quickly.

My First 'Real' Bike Race

A few weeks later, I entered my first 'real' bike race. Another one of my neighbors, John York, had seen a 20-mile bike race advertised in the nearby town of Kinston. John was witnessing all the crazy cycling going on, and he started riding his bike too. We rode together a few times, but he was way behind me in the training category. This didn't stop him from deciding we should enter a bike race that was being advertised in the town of Kinston.

I had been riding for about ten months now. It was the spring of 1985. I was still riding almost every day and could average 20mph for at least two loops, or 13 miles. I had ridden 20 to 25 miles several times. The race in Kinston was a 20-mile event, and John and I both signed up. We figured we had first and second place wrapped up. I was well on my way to the 1988 Olympics by now.

This was actually the first time I had ever ridden off of the Air Force Base. We showed up in Kinston on the morning of the race, and perhaps our hopes were dashed just a little. We quickly realized we were the only ones not wearing lycra. Most of the other folks owned expensive bikes. John and I wore t-shirts and regular shorts. As we checked out the competition, we both realized we might be out of our league.

As we lined up at the start line with about 100 other cyclists, we noticed a rather plump gentleman lining up too; he was short and probably 280 pounds. John took one look and nicknamed him 'Chubby.' He leaned over to me and said, *"Hey, at least we won't finish last!"* We both chuckled.

The gun went off, and away we went. At least a hundred riders were jockeying for position, and I managed to hang with the leaders for about ½ mile. I then watched them power away from me as I pedaled as fast as I could. *"Well, maybe I'll catch up with them,"* I thought. As the ride progressed, though, I realized I had a lot more work to do.

Within the first mile John and I were strung out near the back of the group, and it only got worse from there. I persevered and finished the 20-mile race in about 1 hour and 10 minutes, riding most of the way by myself. I did finish ahead of perhaps 25 others, including John. Kay and my kids were there at the finish line cheering for me. I joined them a moment after finishing, and we watched the remaining riders trickling in. Where was John? Finally, about 15 minutes later, we saw him approaching the finish.

The race ended with an uphill climb, and John was fighting it out with Chubby! *"Come on, John!"* we all screamed as we were watching the final riders struggling to make it up the hill. Lucky for John, he nipped Chubby by about an inch at the finish line. If not, he'd have never heard the end of it. As far as I can remember, that was the last time John ever climbed aboard a bicycle.

I stayed for the awards ceremony and ended up chatting with the winner. He turned out to be a former runner turned cyclist, named Frank Drohan from Goldsboro. That was the beginning of a friendship that has endured for 35 years, and Frank remains today as one of my very best friends in this world. I'm quite certain his name will appear many times in the pages of my books. He is a one-of-a-kind man!

While I was disappointed with my performance in Kinston, I wasn't deterred. I was determined to get better. The race in Kinston had been my first experience with riding in a group. For almost a year, I had been doing most all my riding by myself. The race had given me a taste of what it was like to draft off another cyclist, and I had quickly learned it helped a lot to have somebody in front of me to cut through the wind. I'd never thought of looking for a group to ride with, but a seed was planted.

The Seyboro Club!

The weeks rolled by, and I continued riding. I was getting faster by the day and gradually got to the point where I was riding an average of 20 mph or better every time I rode. I started increasing my distances but remained on base for all of my riding. The speed limit for cars on the base was 25 mph, and a lot of my route was on relatively remote roads, so I didn't have to worry too much about traffic or perhaps being hit by a car. By now, I was about a year into my new hobby, and I began thinking about finding a group to ride with. I had not heard about any bike clubs on the base or in the adjacent city of Goldsboro. It was sporadic to ever see somebody else on a bike. Somehow, though, I thought there had to be others who enjoyed cycling as much as I did.

About a year after I began riding, Kay noticed an article in our local newspaper. It announced a meeting for anyone interested in forming a local bike club in the Goldsboro area. Finally, it was a chance I had been looking for; to help form a local club. The next thing I know is I showed up for the meeting a couple of days later and met with about 5 or 6 other men. These were some men who became lifelong friends. Among them were Rick Sessions, who continues to ride with me to this day. Several others, including Brian Brothers, Walt Hamlin, and Randall Rigsby, were in attendance and, along with Rick and me, who would ultimately become big contributors to the formation of the club.

Soon, everyone started to notice our existence. A new bike shop, 'Bicycle World,' was just opening in Goldsboro, and the Quality Bike Shop was already in business. Shop owners Mike Wiggins and Richard Synger, both offered to do whatever they could to help our club grow and prosper. About the same time, a large Goldsboro Family YMCA facility opened on the north side of town. They saw the potential in us and expressed their interest in helping our club grow. You could say that in the summer of 1985, the stars were all aligned in our favor.

Coming up with a name for the club proved to be a challenge. We all sat down and started with the mind-mapping. Some guys wanted the name 'Goldsboro' to be used. A few of us Air Force men wanted Seymour Johnson Air Force Base to resonate in our club's name somehow, but none of the names seemed to be intriguing enough. During our discussion, somebody mentioned the acronym

'Seyboro,' and since then, this is what we call ourselves, and this is how our club, *the Seyboro Cyclists*, was born.

Today, the club is almost 35 years old, and I am happy to announce that we have Seyboros all over the world. We have seen many things happen during these years of togetherness, including at least four marriages between members who met on our rides. We have seen eight or more children being born from those unions, and they are Seyboros by birth. Extremely close friendships have evolved and continue to evolve to this day. We never imagined that 35 years later, we would still be a club, riding together, and enjoying a reputation as one of the friendliest bike clubs in existence.

I'm happy to say that cycling helped my original goal to lose weight. That, however, is not all it did. It helped me better up myself, my life, and the lives of those around me, which is much more than I had ever imagined. I have made a completely new family other than my original family, and I call them Seyboros. I have learned and explored many things throughout this journey. I learned to work hard and not give up and push through the sweat and pain to reach the next level. Most importantly, I have learned that nothing in this world is impossible to achieve if you are determined.

It all starts with an inspiration, which becomes a goal for you to achieve. We all know that to achieve our goals, we have to break the barriers by putting in our efforts, and that is something I did nonstop.

Seyboro Memory

"Not saying that Frank Drohan, Rick Sessions, George Howell and I have been riding for a long time. But we used to stop in this store near Kenly and buy a Coca-Cola for a nickel, then get 2 pennies back for returning the bottles!"

Chapter 3
Seyboro is Born

The name was decided, people were there, and the Seyboro club was born. Although just a small number of people were part of the group initially, we left our first meeting in a new state of mind. Few of the guys who were part of the meeting had been riding with a group before called Goldsboro cyclists, but it was never a formal organization. This time, things were different. Seyboro was not going to be any ordinary group of people that we knew for sure.

Before we left our first meeting, we had planned on meeting again in a week and share some ideas for the growth and management of our new club. At first, we approached Mike and Rick, the owners of both bike shops in town. We gave them our club's name and some initial thoughts that we had for the promotion. To our surprise, both men were instrumental in promoting and spreading the word. We also spoke with Kriquette Davis at the Family Y, a nonprofit organization, serving the people of Wayne County. She promised to help promote us, which was yet another good news for us. The grapevine was up and running.

Seyboro Club's Second Meeting

The best part of it all was we nearly doubled in numbers in our second meeting, which was just a week later. I don't remember everyone who showed up at the second meeting, but I do remember Frank Drohan, who I had met at the bike race in Kinston. Others who were present involved Greg Shugar and his girlfriend, Kathy. Another accomplished cyclist and runner, Steve Thomas, showed up as well. Anyone could easily feel the excitement present in the air. It seemed as though our idea of a club would rock, and everyone present in the room were equally willing to partake in its growth.

Anyway, the meeting began, and we elected a few people, perhaps officers, for a formal start. Greg took charge of this project; he was a great organizer. We also planned our group's first group ride. Only the thought of it was so exciting that none of us could wait for it.

Seyboro Club's First Group Ride

All of our group members gathered at Bicycle World on

Ash Street, near the center of Goldsboro, for our first ride. At 6:00 PM, our group of about twelve Seyboros headed west on Ash Street. The traffic was somewhat more massive than usual, but we made it through to the town and onto Ash Street extension, riding towards Cherry Hospital and Stevens Mill Road.

It was my first ever 'group' ride if I do not count the one I had taken part in Kinston. Soon I found out I was not the only one. It was the first group ride for many of us, which was evident because most participants ran into issues. We were a group of people with different skill levels, from some fast riding folks to some who were apprehensive and rather slow. I felt I was somewhere in the middle. I had been riding for a year, which is why I possessed somewhat strong bike handling skills, but I surely was not familiar with group riding techniques.

Group Riding Techniques

Let me explain a little more about group riding. In a perfect world, under favorable circumstances, one can enjoy an ideal group ride. This is because, for a perfect ride, all cyclists must have very similar skills and strength. As the ride progresses, the riders take turns at the front. It takes extra effort to lead a group. As I explained earlier, the wind has a lot to do with cycling; therefore, whoever is leading the group is also breaking the wind for the ones behind.

The leader is also responsible for letting everyone know if there is any red signal ahead, for instance, potholes, sand, and glass. The riders following try to stay close to each other, enough to take advantage of drafting and staying somewhat out of the wind. They try and maintain sufficient distance to not touch the wheels of the cyclist in front of them. This typically spells disaster for the one at the back, as it will often cause them to lose control and crash. This subsequently causes trouble for all the cyclists behind and can result in a massive pile-up. I hope by following these techniques, we can avoid such crashes.

The group moves along at a pace comfortable for each participant. The rider in the front stays there for a moment or so, then signals that they're ready to drop off. That's when another cyclist takes the lead. The leader would simply drift to their left, allowing the other riders to pass by, and then fall in at the back of the group. Once they are back in line, they stay out of the wind and slowly start working their way to the front again. This loop continues, as each rider takes a turn and drops back.

By riding in a pace-line like this, the riders stay fresh and active. The reason behind it is that it's no longer the responsibility of a single person to maintain the momentum; everyone works together. It's also a great way for a group of riders to eat up some miles. Another benefit of a pace-line is that it gives weak riders a chance to stay in the back if necessary, without being noticed. Instead of rotating through and taking turns at the front, they can stay at the back of the group and avoid the wind.

In the beginning, our club had no clue what we were doing, but as time passed by, our club kept improving and developed tremendous skills at this type of riding. In a nutshell, our first group ride was a rodeo. We ended up with some cyclists way down the road, others in the middle, and some bringing up the rear. It was more like four to five separate groups riding together, each busy doing their own thing. Somehow, though, we all made it safely back to Bicycle World, and we couldn't stop talking about the fun we had along the way. It was beginning to look like the Seyboro cyclists had already become a family, and we knew we were going to survive and grow as a club.

How the Family Expanded

The word began to spread like a fire in woods, and soon, we started to pick up some new riders. Back in those days, Goldsboro had more than 40,000 residents; Wayne County consisted of over 100,000, and Seymour Johnson Air Force base had a military population of over 5,000 active people on duty, along with many family members. Quite a few folks were looking for ways to exercise, and we started to see new faces showing up at almost every ride. The Seyboro family was expanding at a fast pace.

Nevertheless, not everyone that showed up was experienced at riding a bicycle. Our club struggled with ways to accommodate, manage, and train people with different skill levels. The group included an array of participants from experienced, fast cyclists, to the new riders who had just bought their first bicycle since childhood. It was obviously a challenge for us to manage them all at once, but once again, Seyboro club proved itself to be the best cycling club in town. Folks continued to come back for the next ride and sometimes brought a prospective new member along with them. As I said earlier, the family was continually growing, which made us all so happy. That's when we decided that it's time we come up with different offers that most people enjoyed. Hence, we began offering group rides two nights a week, as well as on Saturday mornings. We were now a family of 50 members and were still growing with every passing day. Somewhere along the way, somebody came up with the idea of electing officers and developing a charter. I am not sure whose idea it was, but everyone agreed it was a good one. In retrospect, whoever thought it up was not admitting it.

The Family Y was kind enough to offer their facility for Seyboro meetings. The first meeting was in a standing room only. I remember Greg Shugar sort of took charge. By the end of the meeting, we decided to hold monthly meetings, charge a small fee to join the club, charge an annual fee for club dues, and elect officers. Greg offered to write the charter, which would contain a lot of rules, and guidance on club matters. The officers' election took place, and we elected a president, vice president, treasurer, and secretary. Things looked more in place and properly managed this way. Everyone had a responsibility to take care of, and this way, each part of the club was becoming stronger. Now I want to go on record here. I do not remember being elected as the president. That's my story, and I am sticking to it. Other members of the club have been calling me 'The Prez' for 35 years now, but I believe they are mistaken.

Weekly group rides continued to take place twice a week during evenings, but as we grew in numbers, so did the traffic on the road. We were now having groups of 30 or more riders, which is why maneuvering our way through the city streets was getting difficult. It was nearly impossible for us to keep the group together with red lights. Fifteen minutes after leaving Bicycle World, we started hitting the suburbs, and the riders up front would stop and wait for everybody to

catch up. By the end of each ride, we would again face the same issue. As we rode back into the town on the main drag, Ash Street, we encountered heavy traffic, which was so annoying.

"We Want More Rides"

The next monthly meeting took place, and again there was a noticeable number of people. During the meeting, applications were handed out and completed, and dues were collected. We also talked about our weekly scheduled rides. Everybody present in the room was stoked. *"We want more rides,"* they said. This did not leave a choice for us; hence we scheduled a ride from Monday to go on till Thursday, but only during evenings. On Saturday and Sunday, these rides would take place in the morning and afternoons, respectively. Kriquette from Family Y offered us the opportunity to begin and end our rides at her facility. The offer was not bad because Family Y was located on the north side of Goldsboro, and we knew we would encounter much less traffic there. So, we ended up changing our starting location, and we all felt much safer with less traffic in sight. At least now we could enjoy our group rides in a little peace.

The Winter Rides!

It was September by now. Most avid cyclists would agree with me that we began to feel a sense of gloom as we watch the sun go down earlier each evening. Everyone could easily feel a chill in the air. A sense of impending doom enveloped us. By mid-October, with the change from daylight savings time, it would get dark by 5:30 or 6:00 in the evening. This put an end to our weekday rides, at least for those who work a normal schedule. We could still ride on weekends, but we would also have to battle with cold winds and dropping temperatures. This was the real test for the Seyboro club. Can we survive the winter?

We did survive somehow. As the evenings grew shorter, and the temperatures dropped every day, we started seeing fewer and fewer riders. Our monthly meetings stopped taking place after October. It was time for hardcore cyclists to come forth. About 8 to 10 of us continued to ride on weekends through that first winter of 1985.

Though it was tough, we had a lot to learn about cold-weather cycling. Soon we realized that clothing designed for cold-weather cycling was a must but expensive for sure. Nonetheless, we obviously did not give in. We would keep riding and sometimes finish a ride with frozen snot on our faces, along with fingers and toes that we could barely feel. Ice would cover the beards of those who had facial hair. The passion that we witnessed during those days was insane. Were we crazy? Maybe!

Every Saturday, when I would leave the house at 25 degrees outside, Kay would look at me and say, *"Are you out of your mind?"* Perhaps I was, but to this day, I have never regretted those cold rides. It was the people of our group and their support that kept me motivated. I need to credit our small group of dedicated riders who rode with me, including Frank Drohan, Rick Sessions, Brian Brothers, Walt Hamlin, Steve Thomas, Greg Shugar, Roarke Stewart, and Randall Rigsby. I may be forgetting a name or two out because it was a long time ago, but I applaud this group of dedicated men for keeping the embers glowing through our first winters.

Spring - The end of our monthly meetings

In 1986, when spring arose, our riders began to show up again. It would not be wrong to say that it was just like the flowers and leaves growing back on the trees. A lot of fun, jokes, and teasing each other would go on, just like in a family. The hardcore riders, including me, who had continued to ride through the tough time of winter, gave fair-weather riders a lot to grief, but it was all in fun.

I believe we held our first monthly meeting in April, and everyone was there, pumped up and ready to ride again. When it was time for our next monthly meeting in May, only about three members of the club showed up. Where was everyone? Their cars were parked in the Family Y parking lot, but they were nowhere to be seen. Anyway, we held our meeting and discussed a few important things related to our club. Later, when we were leaving the building, we saw a bunch of our members coming into the parking lot on their bikes. It was easy to figure out they were finishing up a group ride. We went over to speak with them, of course. *"Hey guys, did you forget our meeting,"* I asked. *"No, we didn't,"* they replied. *"But we decided we would much rather ride our bikes than sit through a boring bike club meeting."*

Well, that was nothing big, but it sure put an end to our monthly meetings. By now, our bike club was firmly entrenched. Our numbers grew to over 100 members in the second year, 1986. The word had spread well. People in Goldsboro were taking notes and showing interest. The local newspaper wrote some articles about us as well.

After all, it all began with a newspaper when Kay came across an article related to bicycle club. When I came to attend the first meeting, little did I know that this group of bicyclists would have such a huge impact on my life. I had zero clues that it would become so important to me in the near future that I would be writing a book about it. In my first book, I spoke about deciding to settle in Goldsboro, following my retirement from the air force. There were many reasons why Kay and I took that decision. One of the primary reasons we chose Goldsboro was the bike club, and all of the fun experiences I had with my club members and planned to have in the future.

No one has ever known the future, and I did not know either. This club sure had a positive impact on my life and on my health, but even the negative aspects of it turned out to be positive in the end. I had never imagined encountering a bicycle accident, which I did in 2006. It was an accident that wrecked my body and nearly took my life. The love, attention, and support I received from the Seyboros during that time played a huge role in my survival and recovery from that accident. I can never thank them enough.

A Seyboro Memory

We often picked on Chuck because, well, he was fun to pick on. During one of our Tour de Fools rides, we had all purchased some new water bottles made by Polar. They were insulated to keep our drinks cold for longer. They were available in red and blue. During our ride, Jörg, who doesn't miss much, noticed that everyone had a blue bottle except Chuck, who had red. When we stopped at a store to refill, we would normally fill our bottles half with ice cubes and half with water. This usually worked to keep our drinks cool for an hour or so on really hot days.

At one of our stops, Jörg whispered to all of us (except Chuck) to fill our bottles to the brim with just ice cubes, no water. We did so, and then hit the road. About 90 minutes later, Jörg pulled up next to Chuck and asked, *"How's your bottle working?"* Chuck took a drink and replied, *"Well, the ice is melted, and it's getting warm."* Jörg reached for his bottle and shook it. We could hear the remaining bits of ice rattling in the bottle. He said, *"Well Chuck, you bought the winter bottle, not the summer bottle. It's red, made to keep drinks warm."* Chuck muttered, *"Bullsh**, the bottles are the same."* *"No, they're not, Chuck,"* Jörg replied. *"Guys, check your bottles."*

By now we realized what Jörg was up to, and each of us reached for our bottles and shook them. They all had small amounts of ice left in them and made the distinctive rattling sound. The look on Chuck's face was unforgettable! Had he really bought the winter bottle?

Rumor has it that Chuck went to the bike shop as soon as we got home and ordered some more bottles, specifying that they <u>MUST</u> be blue! Mike, the shop owner, just shook his head and wondered what in the world the Seyboros had told Chuck.

Chapter 4
The Early Days

Life was going on, our club was growing, and we were all learning and exploring things together. Together, we had created our little world where there was no space for the lazy. Our 'band of misfit cyclists' was quickly evolving into a great group of riders; we were pleased about it. As time passed by, the Seyboro family kept growing. I was making a lot of new friends who shared the same passion for cycling that I had found long ago in an unknown place inside myself. When you meet people with similar interests, the conversation never ends, and you become friends even before you know it.

Our Biggest Challenge

The most difficult challenge we faced and continue to face today, even after 35 years, is trying to tailor our rides in a way that all of our members are satisfied. We sure are diverse in terms of many things, and our riders have a wide variety of skills, abilities, and desires. Each one of them has their reason for riding. Some do it because they aim to become competitive to other cyclists, with an eye on future racing. Some do it because they want to get in good physical shape or lose weight, and some do it out of a hobby. Many do it just for the camaraderie of being with a group of like-minded people.

On any given evening or weekend, we would often have 25 or more riders showing up for the group rides. The strongest could ride all evening at speeds well over 20 mph, but others became stressed trying to hold on 18 mph, or even 15 mph. People in our group belonged to different ages, from mid-teens up to folks in their seventies. The biggest question was, how could we hold a ride that would be equally fun, enjoyable, and memorable for all in attendance? It was also the basis of whether we are going to be successful as a club or not. I will tell you what the Seyboro Cyclists did to resolve this issue, and I am proud to say I genuinely think we did it better than most.

In the very beginning, we all rode together as one big group. We were all learning at the same time, but I also mentioned earlier about the nuisances of riding in a group and things that can go wrong if only one person loses control. Anyway, for months, we rode together. The club leaders would often decide on the route before the ride began. We agreed that everyone should not know the route. This way, it will be easier for us to keep everyone on the same page, without losing the fun element.

Hence, only a few of us knew where we were heading. It worked well, better than we had expected because whenever any group members decided they wanted to ride faster and took off from the rest of the group, they would have to stop and wait every time they got to an intersection in front of them. They did not know if the leading group was going to take a turn or go straight.

It was a great way to keep the fast riders in check. At the same time, it did not stop them from having some fun and riding fast at the same time. They only would have to stop and wait for everyone to catch up every few miles.

I would sometimes take off with the fast riders but bring everyone to a stop when we arrived at an intersection. We would wait for the others to catch up. It might sound annoying as you read it, but trust me, even those waiting sessions were such a joy. Evenings make everything look so beautiful. At least this way, we got a chance to feel our surroundings. It also allowed them to take a break and interact with one another, so nobody seemed to mind any of this at all.

Besides, these stops served as an incentive to some of the new riders. After riding with the group for a while and improving their skills, they would sometimes try taking off with the fast folks to see how long and far they could hang with them. In case if they got dropped out in the middle, they knew they wouldn't be left out there all by themselves. There would still be riders bringing up the rear. Moreover, the ones ahead would have to wait at intersection anyway, so they had nothing on the loose.

A New System of Rides

After our rides were well-established, and some additional leaders took the responsibility, we went on to create a new system of rides. According to this new system, we would advertise ahead of time, the fast riders' group, or the casual group. Folks would have a choice whichever group they wanted to be a part of. The fast-riders' group consisted of more robust and experienced riders, and the rule for them was, they would leave about ten minutes before the casual group. The casual group consisted of our other riders who weren't interested in riding faster or were unable to catch up at a faster pace. If somebody tried riding with the fast group and it got above their head, they knew the casual group would be along shortly, so they wouldn't have to finish the ride all by themselves. This system worked well and kept almost everybody satisfied. As a precaution, we would always make sure one of our experienced riders rode with the casual group to assist with any mechanical issues, and to ensure everyone got back to the finishing point in time.

Few of the many problems

We learned a lot through trials and errors we encountered during our journey. These learnings also included some of the most critical issues that road cyclists face today. Though I learned several such things at an early stage, what I learned first was handling flat tires. In chapter 2, I spoke about my many rides on base, back and forth to the firing range, and how during one of my on-base rides, I reached the firing range with a flat tire. I had no spare tube, with no source to connect with anyone I knew. There were no cell phones back in those days, and it was a very remote area. I ended up walking the 3+ miles back home on foot. Now, many serious cyclists wear special shoes with cleats on the sole that clip into the pedals. These pedaling systems help a lot with pedaling efficiency, but they are not made for walking, as many of these shoes include a large plastic or metal cleat on the sole of the shoe near the ball of the foot.

Unfortunately, I was wearing one of those shoes. The walk from firing range to home was more like either try to walk on the cleats or take the shoes off and walk barefoot on the hot asphalt. I ended up using a combination of these options. It was the longest walk I had ever taken home. Before my next ride, I made sure I bought a spare tube and a small pump designed to carry on a bike - lesson learned the hard way!

Similarly, many things can go wrong when riding several miles on the road. It is better to be prepared for any sort of mishap, such as flat tires, dropped or broken chains, gears not shifting correctly, a broken spoke, and saddles not adjusted properly, which are some of the most common problems riders face. We as a club did not only make our members aware of such issues, but also taught them how to resolve them. We took pride in how we would accompany and assist the new and inexperienced members on our rides. We taught them how to fix a flat tire, adjust gear, and lots of other necessary lessons. We were incredibly proud as we watched them develop into strong, capable, and competitive cyclists.

Riding Two-Abreast

It definitely takes leadership skills to guide a group of riders when we are sharing the road with motorists. We rode two-abreast for a reason. When cars approached from the rearm, they often tried to pass a single file line of riders, even with traffic approaching from the other direction. Our rural roads were and still are narrow, with no shoulders. We usually rode about a foot or more to the left of the shoulder. There just wasn't enough room in our lane for a car to pass safely with another car in the opposite lane. Riding two-abreast forced the motorist to wait until the oncoming lane is clear before they try to pass.

We still do encounter the angry motorist from time to time who feel we are holding them up. However, we go great lengths to avoid confrontation, and I am proud to say we, the Seyboros, have had a tremendous 35-year history of sharing the road with Wayne and surrounding counties around Goldsboro, and 99% of the motorists are courteous to us. If you are one of those motorists and reading this book right now, thank you for allowing us to share the roads!

The 'Hammerfest'

By the end of 1986, the Seyboro Cyclists were well organized and, on our way, toward sharing many years of fun, fellowship, and competitiveness. My fondest memories of our evening rides include our Wednesday night rides to Fremont and back. A small group of the really hardcore riders would meet at the Family Y, separate from the fast riders and casual groups. There were usually 6 to 8 of riders present in these races.

We had mapped a 35-mile route that took us into northern Wayne County to the little town of Fremont, where we would stop briefly for a cold drink and be on the bikes again, hell-bent on being the first one back to the Y. These rides were true 'Hammerfest.' If somebody could not hold the pace, they were left behind, facing the long ride home. We would draft off one another and take turns up front. At the same time, we kept a watch for any opportunity to break away from others, particularly on hills along the route. The closer we got to the finishing point, the more vicious the ride became, and each of us was always hell-bent on being the first one back to the finish.

I remember battling things out each Wednesday with Frank Drohan, Brian Brothers, Paul Harrell, Russell Boyce, Dave Scarano, Tim Scott, Steve Thomas, Larry Vaniwarden, and Eric Barnes, among others. We were proud of these rides and would sometimes average 25 mph from start to finish. Bicycling is undoubtedly the only sport where you can curse your competitors for making things difficult for you, but hug them at the end of the ride and look forward to riding with them soon.

From a small club to an organization

In addition to our ride schedule, the bike club began getting together for other reasons as well. We would gather somewhere on a rainy evening to have dinner, which typically included pizza and beer. We would also sometimes get together with our families following a long Saturday ride to eat ice cream and drink Yoo-hoo. At just about any time during the week, we knew if we stopped by the bike shop, there would be fellow club members in there, telling stories or chatting.

This social side of our club was essential to most of the other members and me; we were making friends who would turn out to be lifetime buddies. Cyclists become friends. You know you can count on others for anything, at any given time. In just a short time, our club had grown and matured into a great organization. It consisted of 100 plus members now. The good thing about it was we had a diverse range of people who belonged to different races and ages. It was a mixture of males and females, a few teenagers, and several married couples. In 1986, the club also participated in numerous bicycle events that took place across North Carolina. We would also often travel together with as many as 40 members on board.

Social Corporate Responsibility

I believe that every organization must be socially responsible—one of the reasons why we also began to take on some civic responsibilities. We worked with Family Y, arranging some fundraisers to assist them, and also volunteered to help them with some of their sporting events. We did some work with the North Carolina Bicycle Safety Program by visiting area elementary schools and talking to young children about bike safety. It helped us maintain our reputation as well as earn some good deeds. Our image as a happy, friendly, and well-rounded bunch of cyclists began to spread and remain the same. I am so proud that I helped create this group of amazing cyclists who believe in growing together and working for the society.

A Seyboro Memory

That one member we could not beat!

In the late 1980s when Frank was the top dog in our club, we looked for ways to slow him down. On a Saturday ride about 25 miles from home, we stopped at a store to get some drinks. Frank then asked if we could wait an extra minute or so while he went to use the bathroom. While he was gone, we tightened the rear brake pads on Frank's bike. This is easy to do. All you need to do is turn the adjusting barrel until the brake pads are rubbing against the wheel. We tightened them quite a bit; enough that the wheel would not spin freely but would spin under some pressure.

Frank came out, got on his bike, and we headed toward home. Several times, Frank commented that it felt like we were riding into a headwind, he was working pretty hard. We never told him what we had done to his bike. I guess he will find out when he reads this. The irony is, he still beat us in the final sprint when we got back home!

Unbeatable Frank Drohan with Diesel Dave

Chapter 5
The Harvest Hundred

1987 was the year filled with lots of fun and excitement, for this was the year when our bike club entered the upcoming riding season. I was one of the hardcore riders who continued to ride throughout the winters and looking back now, I cannot help but wonder how we even managed to do it. Although the winters in Eastern North Carolina are probably mild compared to the rest of the country, yet there are many nights when the temperature is in the 20s, strong winds blow from the north.

There were many Saturday mornings that I had to suck it up, dress warmly, and head for Family Y. I would always come across five or more riders, each one of us complaining about the adverse weather conditions, yet were all filled with passion and determination. It sure was a commendable sight. When spring finally arrived, we were in better shape than the fair-weather folks, and a lot of good-natured ribbing was going on with the members who had sat out the winter. It was always fun to pull their leg on what they had missed.

Seyboro Sponsoring 'The Harvest Hundred'

In the early part of 1987, one of our club leaders, Greg Shugar, came up with the idea of the Seyboro Cyclists sponsoring a century ride. It sounded like a great idea to everyone, and it indeed was a good one. Hence, without a second thought, we all joined heads and started making plans to execute it. We would give ourselves plenty of time to map out a route, and hold the ride in the latter part of the summer of every fall.

As I mentioned in the previous chapter, we scheduled some meetings to discuss the ride, even though many of our members hated attending meetings. They liked to be outside riding rather than sitting in a room and talking. But we had enough club leaders to get together, and we came up with a plan. We decided that we would call this ride 'the Harvest Hundred,' and we would hold it on the 1st Saturday in October.

Deciding the Route

I remember Greg seemed to have the rare talent of organizing things the best way, so he took the lead role in organizing the ride. We started spending our Saturdays making various trips around Wayne County and the surrounding area to find an acceptable route for the ride. After a considerable amount of riding and planning, we came up with a route that would take us to the four corners of Wayne County and into neighboring Johnston County. We would start and finish at the Goldsboro Family Y. The total distance was 101 miles. It was a beautiful route and took us in a lot of the small towns inside and around Wayne County while keeping us on rural roads for the entire distance.

We decided to offer a 50-mile ride, and a 25-mile ride as well for those who were not up to doing the century. Even I had doubts about riding a century. I had ridden one century before this and had ridden as many as 75 miles on several occasions. But I had the entire summer ahead of me to prepare for the first annual Harvest Hundred. I knew I would have to be in good shape to contend with the challenge, and I also knew I had the potential. We were calling it a ride, of course. But as said before, when several people ride together, it turns into a race for many of us.

The Looka Hill

The roads in Wayne County are relatively flat. We have some small, short hills, and some of them may be a 5% grade but not more than a couple of hundred yards long. When folks from the mountains came and rode with us, they would laugh at us when we talked about our hills. *"Those aren't hills,"* they would say. *"Come out to Asheville, and we will show you some real hills."* But even a small hill can make a difference in a competitive bike ride. Somebody can sprint away at the beginning of a climb and catch the other riders by surprise. If that person has been riding smart, staying at the back of the pack, and not taking too many pulls, they might just be able to open up a gap on the rest of the group. Our very own, Frank Drohan, was well-known for this tactic, and we managed to incorporate a few of our area's biggest hills into the route. Most famous among them, of course, was 'Looka Hill.'

We were riding west on Hinnant-Edgerton Road in Johnston County about 30 miles into the route. It was one of our scouting rides when we were trying to find an excellent course for the Harvest Hundred. At one point, Brian Brothers said, *"Hey, look, a hill!"* Sure enough, straight up the road in front of us was a rather steep hill, climbing up out of sight into the trees. We had not been on this road before and were surprised to see a hill of this magnitude.

Of course, we all took off to see who could be the first one to the top. It was a rather tough climb for our part of eastern North Carolina. We all made a mental note of this point. This would be a good place to try and break away from the main group when we rode the Harvest Hundred. Perhaps shake off any riders from other clubs who were still riding with the leaders at that point.

It is always good to be prepared about the consequences rather than waiting until we experience them. So, not long before the ride, several of us went out in our cars and on motorcycles to mark the route. Of course, we had to examine each and everything before the big day. We would paint arrows at each of the intersections where a turn was required. Much to our surprise, as we were approaching 'Looka Hill,' we saw that somebody from the club was out there before us. In big, bold letters stretching across the road at the start of the hill, they had painted in large letters, 'LOOKA HILL!' It was so that we could see it from a distance and prepare for putting pressure on our legs. This piece of road with Looka

Hill has been a talking point in our club ever since we discovered it. We even went out periodically to freshen the paint so that it remained prominent in our club history. I just hope I am not getting myself in trouble with the DOT!

Advertisement of the Ride

By this point, everything seemed to be in a perfect rhythm. The feelings of Seyboros were a mixture of excitement and nervousness. We advertised the ride with the NC Bicycle Safety Group, sent out flyers to all of the bike shops within about a hundred miles, and handed out flyers at other area rides we attended throughout the summer. We also had t-shirts printed for the participants. We had SAG stops planned for the 25, 50, and 75-mile points, along with a roving SAG vehicle to be on the course. Some of our club and family members also volunteered to man the SAG stops. Everything seemed to be in perfect rhythm, and we were all ready to make history.

The Big Day

The day of the ride finally arrived. Most of the participants showed up at 7 AM, but the ride was not scheduled to start until 8 AM. The atmosphere on site was a beautiful sight to witness. It was as if a festival was going on, and it was not at 7 in the morning but evening. Everyone present was excited and cheerful. About 50 of our club members had signed up to do the ride, and we had almost 50 participants from out-of-town. For the club's first organized ride, we were all happy with the turnout. The weather was beautiful. Light winds out of the northwest were blowing, and temperatures were peaking at about 75 degrees. It was a typical day of fall in Wayne County.

At about 8 AM, all the participants gathered at the starting point in front of the Family Y. A hundred cyclists gathered together is quite a sight. One of our members led the group in a short prayer for safety. We had arranged for a patrol deputy with the local Sheriff's office to lead us out for the first mile to get us safely through a few busy intersections. Somebody with a bull horn announced, *"Riders Ready? Go!"* And off we went!

We offered three different distances for the ride completion; 25, 50, and 100 miles. All participants of the three routes started at the same point for the first 10 miles, where the 25-mile participants had to make a turn to begin their return back home. The remainder of the riders would continue to ride the same route for the first 30 miles. At this point, the 50-milers would make a left turn to begin their journey back, and the hundred-milers would continue straight. Registrations indicated about 75 of the riders planned to do the century, but it was nice to have an option. Perhaps somebody headed out from the beginning with the plan to do 100 miles. But by the time they were 30 miles into the ride, and they realized it would be too much for them, and it would be difficult for them to make it, so they could take the turn and return via the 50-mile course.

The Race Begins!

It was not so long into the ride when the 'race' began. A few strong riders took off from the pack. The rest of us watched for a few minutes and then realized if we didn't give a chase, they might stay away for the entire ride. So about 20 of the stronger riders banded together and gave chase. Here is where team tactics start to play a role. If the leaders are riding at 23mph, we will have to ride at 24 or 25mph to catch them. The key is to take short pulls at the front, drop off and let the next person take a turn. Then, get the pace up to about

25 and take short pulls. With 20 riders, nobody has to work too long at the front. That's precisely what we did, and within a few minutes, we had reeled in the leaders.

There were now perhaps 25 of us riding in the lead pack. Most were Seyboros, with maybe about 5 or 6 belonging to other bike clubs. We rode along at a pretty good clip, testing each other's abilities and strengths. We zoomed on past the 25-mile SAG stop. Everyone still had plenty of water, and if anyone had stopped at that point, the others would not have waited for them.

We Seyboros knew we would be hitting Looka Hill in just a few miles and hence planned to try and break up the pack at that point. Just shy of 30 miles, we started up Looka Hill. Frank Drohan started things, as he usually did. You could just tell by looking at him that he is acting the most typical of himself. I watched him closely, and as soon as he came out of the saddle, I started accelerating.

Seven others went with us; all of them were Seyboros. As we opened up a small gap on the other riders, the people behind us cussed and hollered, but we were determined. Any experienced cyclist can tell you about the pain and suffering we sometimes endure to reach a goal or a milestone while riding. On that day in October of 1987, nine people were prepared and willing to hurt themselves to open a gap on the other riders while climbing that hill. By the time we reached the top of Looka Hill, we had probably opened a gap of 20 yards on the next closest rider. But we weren't in the clear yet.

There were nine of us, and perhaps nine remaining in the group chasing behind us. It was now a matter of who wanted to win the most. There were still 70 miles to go, and a lot can happen during those long miles. But our group was now made up of 9 Seyboros who had been riding and training together for two years. It was our club's inaugural organized ride. We had to have one of our members finish first. Heaven forbid an out-of-towner take home the win, that wasn't happening!

So, we put the hammer down and rode as fast and as smart as we could. We slowly watched the gap between our two groups grow. From 50 to 100, and then 150 yards, we were making progress. A key to breaking the chase group's spirit in a situation like this is to get far enough ahead so that they can no longer see you. That was going to be tough to do on the roads we were riding; there were long stretches of straight, flat roads. After we made it through the town of Princeton, we started hitting a few turns and roads with some curves. At about 40 miles into the ride, we had gained enough of a lead they could no longer see us. For all they knew, we were 10 miles ahead!

The troubled Race of the Two!

Frank and I were doing most of the work at the front of our group. At one point, he asked, *"How're you feelin' Davie?"* to which I replied, *"Great!"* He told me to stay close to him, and I knew what was going on in his head. As expected, on the next short hill, Frank came out of the saddle and sprinted away. I jumped with him, and in a short time, we had opened up a gap on the others. You should have heard the yelling and cursing that went on this time! *"Hey, what the he**? We're all on the same team."* *"Are you guys crazy?"* *"You'll never get away with this!"* *"I thought we were teammates!"* The fact is, though, we did get away with it. Slowly but surely, Frank and I rode away from our friends and teammates, just as we had done at the top of Looka Hill.

I remember riding east on the Old Smithfield Highway, Frank and I taking short pulls, looking behind, and seeing our friends trying to catch us. Dave Scarano, Wally Acres, Russell Boyce, Paul Harrel, Brian Brothers, and two others. That sight is etched in my brain forever! The anger and rage could be felt even from such a distance, and if looks could kill, Frank and I would have been dead that day! But he and I were determined at this point. I have got to admit, Frank was stronger than me, and he took longer pulls than I did. But we slowly opened up a reasonable gap.

Frank had a riding style that nearly got him in trouble more than once. When he was riding hard and concentrating, he rode with his head down, looking mostly at his front wheel. Many times, when Frank was leading our group, somebody would have to warn him about a car or other obstruction in the road ahead, or he probably would have ridden right into it. I often joke with him about the many times I have saved his life.

Anyway, his riding style got us both in trouble with this first Harvest Hundred. Heading east on Stevens Mill Road, we were supposed to turn south onto Falling Creek Church Road. There were several arrows painted on the road, but

Frank was hammering away with his head down and fixated on his riding. He missed the arrows. I was concentrating on holding Frank's wheel, and I missed the arrows too. We hammered away, utterly ignorant of the fact we had missed a turn.

Several minutes later, I told Frank I thought we should have taken a right turn by now. We continued to ride for another minute or so. I was somewhat familiar with the course, as I had helped paint the arrows on the route. I became convinced, for sure, that we had missed the turn. So, we made the next right turn and discussed how we would get back on the course. We knew there was another road ahead that would take us back to the road we were supposed to be on. We eventually got back on course, but we had ridden about 4 miles out of our way.

The disappointing fact was, we were no longer in the lead. We had burned an extra 10 to 12 minutes, and we knew at least one, if not both, chase groups would now be in front of us, and they didn't even know it! Frank, in his typical mindset, put his head down and started hammering again. He said, *"C'mon Dave. We're gonna catch those guys!"* I said, *"Frank, how are we gonna do that?"* to which he replied,

"We'll never know if we don't try." And with these words coming out of Frank's mouth, we hammered on.

Are we too ahead or too behind?

I have such vivid memories of this ride so clearly that the feelings I had back then can be felt even today. My short-term memory isn't too good, but I remember things about this ride as if it happened yesterday. Frank kept urging me on. We took turns at the front and watched the miles roll by. We kept hoping to see some riders up ahead, but they didn't appear.

We entered the small town of Dudley and knew the 75-mile SAG stop was just ahead after we crossed the railroad tracks. We had both started with five water bottles, and we each had one remaining. That should get us to the finishing point without having to stop. We slowed for the tracks; they were slightly rough and could easily cause a pinch flat. As we started to pick up our speed, we passed a narrow dirt road on our right with a table, water jugs and fruit, and a group of cyclists laying around in the grass. Frank said, *"Dave, that's them!"* They heard Frank, and the melee began. *"How'd they get behind us?"* one of the guys shouted. *"Hurry up!*

We can catch them," shouted another. As Frank and I hammered away, we saw banana peels and cookie wrappers flying as the guys scrambled to get back on their bikes. Frank and I were looking at a gift horse in the mouth and took every advantage of the circumstances. As tired as we were, we found the power to ride away from them one more time. A lot of it is about mental attitude. A strong will plays a vital role in making you escape the hurdles. How badly can I hurt myself to keep in front of these guys? Like we had done earlier during the ride, Frank and I rode away from the chase group. By the time we got just past Seven Springs, we could no longer see them behind us.

All's Well that Ends Well!

We powered the rest of the way, just the two of us. And of course, Frank beat me across the finishing line. It was no surprise. I was delighted to finish the way I did. We hung around and cheered for the rest of the riders as they came to the finish. There was a lot of ribbing and arguing, while some riders were cussing too. But when all is said and done, there was nothing wrong with the way we had ridden. That's how bicycling works! And at the end of the day, we all remain best of friends and promise to kick each other's' butts the next time around.

We continued to host the Harvest Hundred as an organized event for about ten more years. Even after we discontinued holding the organized event, our club members continued to ride the route over the years. We had some great times and some fond memories attached to it that we wanted to relive. Future winners included Karl Gerschutz, Scott Summers, Brian Brothers, Paul Harrell, Mike Haney, Chuck Hand, and Jörg Wagner, to name a few. Our other Seyboros were all strong, faithful riders who often participated and were always a pleasure to ride with. Every one of them was a strong contender.

I talked in my first book about missing the 1990 Harvest Hundred because I was deployed to the war zone. When I made it home in 1991, my son Nick was just ready to turn 12 years old. He expressed an interest in riding with me, so we decided to get him in shape for the Harvest 50. We spent about five months in training, and I experienced some of my best times ever on a bike. I was out there with my only son, watching him grow stronger and faster. It was a wonderful and emotional experience for me.

The Harvest 50 Ride of 1991

In early October 1991, Nick and I entered the 50-mile ride with lots of excitement and trepidation. Would he be able to finish it? I had a feeling that he could. We left 10 minutes before the official start, figuring the hammerheads would catch us before too long. As we headed out together, I realized we had a rather strong tailwind. I didn't mention this to Nick because I did not want him to be discouraged. We had a perfect time, and the lead pack didn't catch up with us until we were 20 miles into the ride. As they whizzed past, they hollered lots of encouragement to Nick. He was feeling good at this point, and I was so proud of him. Imagine a twelve years old kid attempting a 50-mile bike ride! Astonishing, isn't it?

He struggled a little bit as we climbed Looka Hill, but he made it to the top, aided somewhat by the tailwind. As soon as we crested the hill, though, we turned south. We were slightly more than halfway through but were now facing the wind. The remainder of the ride would be difficult.

I got up the front and just urged Nick to hold my wheel. We struggled on for miles, fighting the wind. Our average speed began to plummet. Nick began to complain. About halfway back, he started asking me how much further we had to go. *"How much further, Dad?"* *"Well, Nick, we've gone 42 miles."* After what seemed an eternity to him, he would ask again, *"How much further, Dad?"* and I would say, *"We've gone 42.4 miles, Nick!"* It was like having him in the back seat of the car, as he usually shouts, *"Are we there yet? Are we there yet?"* But I will give my son credit, he hung tough, and we kept pedaling.

Little did Nick know that the route was more than 52 miles? As we crossed over Tommy's Road, he asked me, *"How far have we gone, Dad?"* to which I responded, *"49.2 miles."* A moment later, we passed a point where somebody had painted, 'Only three more miles!' while marking the route. To this day, I can hear Nick screaming at me! In his 12-year-old mind, he had believed we were within a mile of the finishing point. When he saw 'Only three more miles,' it may have been equivalent to three hundred miles for him at that point.

I gave and still give him credit, nonetheless. I appreciated him as he hung tough, and we finished about 15 minutes later. I was so proud of him, and he was proud of himself. What an accomplishment! That gave Nick a head-start on his bicycling journey, which carried him through college and beyond. I had some of my best times with Nick on our bike rides, and I proudly watched as he grew into one of our club's fastest riders. He eventually improved to where he could outride his old man, and I was proud to see him do it!

All is fair in love, war, and bicycling!

As I grew older and suffered some bad injuries, I took over the role of SAG driver. Of course, I had to give up on riding the Harvest Hundred, but I could not keep myself entirely away from it. It was fun to be on the course with the men and women struggling to get ahead, even though I wasn't on the bike. I loved to witness the enthusiasm and passion they brought to the field.

Though even as the SAG driver, I have been accused of 'cheating.' Sometimes I have offered to carry water bottles for the riders; with that being said, those bottles were never seen again! Or even worse, I would give some of their bottles to somebody else. I have been known to motor pace a struggling rider so he or she could get back with the lead pack, and I occasionally would accompany the lady riders on the route and abandon the men; let them fend for themselves!

The ladies were a lot more fun, but hey; all is fair in love, war, and bicycling!

A Seyboro Memory

When I was working for the State Motorcycle Safety Education Program my office was in the small town of Snow Hill, North Carolina. Snow Hill is a small, quaint little town with a bunch of nice folks. And most folks know almost everyone else in town. There is a Fast Break restaurant and gas station which was a normal hangout for folks in the mornings. They had the best cheese biscuits money could buy. You could feel your arteries hardening as you ate them, but they were well worth the risk of a heart attack!

A lot of the folks in Snow Hill knew me from working with the motorcycle safety program, and they often saw me on a motorcycle around town. And I often frequented the Fast Break on Monday mornings, buying cheese biscuits for Carol, John and me. One Monday morning in June, I ran into a friend who was equally interested in giving himself a heart attack with a cheese biscuit. We were making small talk as we waited, and he asked me what I'd done over the weekend.

"I've got to brag on myself a little", I said. "I rode my bike 200 miles on Saturday." He looked at me and replied, "Man, that's a long ride on a motorcycle." I commenced to correct him, saying, "I wasn't on a motorcycle, I was on a bicycle." He looked at me like I was speaking in tongues! "For sure, no you didn't" he said. "I sure did", I replied.

He got a look on his face as they handed him his biscuit and he bid me goodbye. I know to this day he thinks I was lying to him.

Chapter 6
Mountain Riding

I believe it was in 1987 that I discovered several of my fellow Seyboros had participated in the annual "Assault on Mount Mitchell". It was during one of our rides in the early spring and the conversation came up. I was awestruck! Both Frank and Greg had done the ride in a previous year. Both of them immediately went to the top of my list as cyclists I wanted to emulate.

In bicycling, there are certain rides that draw the attention of bicycling magazines and a lot of avid cyclists. The Assault on Mount Mitchell is such a ride. It starts in in Spartanburg, South Carolina. The first 70 miles take the riders through a lot of rolling hills going north towards Marion, North Carolina. At the 50-mile point the route goes up over "Bill's Hill", which seems more like Bill's mountain, because it's a truly steep climb. Thankfully it only lasts a mile, but it gives the riders a hint of what lies ahead. At 74 miles there is a huge SAG stop at an RV park. This is actually the stopping point for many of the riders. From Marion, the route starts the climb up to the Blue Ridge Parkway, and eventually to the top of Mount Mitchell. This mountain is the highest point east of the Mississippi River at 6,684 feet. The Assault on Mount Mitchell finishes at the summit of the mountain, and the total ride distance is 102 miles. The route contains so many climbs that finishers will have climbed vertically more than 10,000 feet by the time they reach the top. The ride has been named one of the 10 most difficult rides in the United States by several bicycling magazines.

Over the years the ride became so popular that the number of entrants overwhelmed the Park Police on the Blue Ridge Parkway. In recent years, they've had to cap the total number of participants at about 800 riders. Since then the ride organizers added the Assault on Marion. There's no limit on the number of riders who leave Spartanburg, SC. It's normally over 2,000 cyclists. But without a ticket to the top, riders must stop at Marion. Don't take this ride lightly though; it is 74 miles with a lot of hills to climb!

I had heard and read a lot about the Assault on Mt Mitchell since the time I first started riding a bike. It was one of those events I'd dreamed of doing but wondered if I would ever be at that level. When I found out that Frank and Greg had done the ride, I started picking their brains. I'd been riding with both of them for several years now and felt I was at their level of fitness. Perhaps I could do it!

When I made up my mind to give it a try, I also encouraged some of my fellow Seyboros to join me in May of 1988. Most of us had no idea what we were getting into but we felt up to the challenge. We trained hard in the early spring and picked Frank's and Greg's brains about what lay ahead. Our biggest worry, living in the flatlands, was how to train for riding long hills. Frank recommended riding into headwinds as much as we could. And we did. We purposely headed out on the windy days and rode into the wind as long and as fast as we could. We developed several popular comments that we use to this day, "The wind is my friend" and "I love the wind". We also found the few hills in our area and practiced riding up them as hard and fast as we could.

We also needed to adjust gears on our bikes. Back then, we were riding bikes with 2 chainrings on the front and 6 cogs on the back, for 12 speeds total. In those days most bikes had front chainrings of 52 and 42 teeth, and a cassette on the back with 6 cogs between 13 and 25 teeth. Our lowest gear would be the 42-25 combination. This gear may work OK for the pros, but us mere mortals would probably need lower gearing. The first year I did the Assault, the best I could do was find a 28-tooth cog for the rear. This gave me a relatively low gear, but nothing like the low gearing that's available nowadays. When I first made the change to my bike, I put it in the lowest gear, the 42-28, and pedaled down the road, wondering how anybody would ever need a gear this low! I was pedaling really fast but barely moving forward. I would find out in a few months!

In late May of 1988, our group headed out on what was unquestionably our most exciting road trip to date; we were on our way to ride the Assault. It was about a 6-hour drive from home, so we left the day prior. When we arrived, we registered at the downtown auditorium in Spartanburg. There were lots of people there, riders and vendors, and lots of story-telling and excitement in the air. When people asked us where we were from and we said "Goldsboro", their normal comment was, "Man, you flat-landers are never gonna make it." This didn't do much for our state of mind, because we all had our doubts already. But we were planning on finishing, no matter what.

On Sunday morning the ride began at 7am. There's nothing like the site of 2,000 bicyclists lined up on the main drag of Spartanburg waiting for the starting gun. We were near the back of the group, and once we got started, it was an awesome sight to see the long, long line of riders stretching out in front of us. There were several low speed crashes as cyclists touched wheels in the confined space, but our group safely made it through the beginning jitters. With me were Frank Drohan and Greg Shugar who'd both done the ride before. Newbies besides me included Brian Brothers, Dave Scarano, Rick Synger, and a few others whose names I've forgotten. We tried to stay together but in a group of that many cyclists we eventually got split up. Each of us found a group that was riding at a pace comfortable for us and we hammered towards Marion.

The ride is well-supported with SAG stops every 10 miles and several SAG vehicles. The rolling hills of the first 75 miles will take a lot out of a person and it only gets worse after that. There was normally a small number of professional riders who entered just for training, and there were quite a few of the top-notch amateur cyclists from around the country who entered as well. First place finishers normally completed the ride in about 5 hours. How they did that, climbing those mountains, I'll never know! The ride organizers do have some time limits. I think back then people had as much as 12 hours to finish.

Once we passed Marion, we started up Highway 80 which took us to the Blue Ridge Parkway. It was somewhere on this road that the climbing became intense. We passed Lake Tahoma, riding along on a slight uphill section, and I remember thinking, "Heck, this isn't so bad. What's all the talk about?!" Then, in the blink of an eye, I was out of the saddle, down into my lowest gear (the 42-28 I spoke of earlier), and barely able to turn the pedals. I kept trying to shift to a lower gear but it wasn't gonna happen, I was already there! And for the next 22 miles I stayed in that lowest gear except for one or two short downhill sections. I remember making the turn off the Parkway onto the final road to the top. A lady on the side of the road hollered, "Good Job! Keep going, it's only 5 more miles!" I looked down at my computer and was doing 4mph, and I thought, "Oh my God, it's gonna take me another hour!"

I made it to the top, crossing the finish line in 8 hours. It took me 4 hours to complete the 75 miles to Marion, and another 4 hours to ride the last 27 miles. This had been, by far, the toughest physical event I had ever accomplished.

Frank, Brian and Greg finished well ahead of me. Our entire group of 'Seyboro Flatlanders' made it across the finish line which was remarkable in itself. As many as a third of the starters fail to finish the ride.

Our minds do funny things sometimes. I sat at the top of Mount Michell, freezing to death. The temperatures at that altitude are much colder. I finally boarded a bus for the ride back to Spartanburg. There was a lot of talk, and a lot of fatigue. I remember telling someone I was glad I'd done the ride but had no plans to ever try again. "Been there, done that." But as the days turn into weeks and weeks into months, somehow our minds forget about the pain and agony of the ride. We only remember the sense of accomplishment we gain when we conquer the mountain. And before I knew it, I was planning on doing the ride again in 1989 with a self-imposed goal of completing in less than 7 hours.

This started a club custom that goes on to this day. Every year there have been Seyboros at the starting line and at the finish. A lot of challenging, bragging, and boasting goes on between the members. We've had as many as 20 Seyboros lined up in Spartanburg. And we've had some strong finishers. Karl Gerschutz and my son, Nick, have both finished in about 5 ½ hours. Frank Drohan has finished under 6 hours. Mike Luke, Tim Shockley, Doug Pearson, Sarah Alholm, Chuck Hand, Paige Christianson.... All have had impressive finishing times. My best time was 6:20, and I finished in that time several years in a row, right alongside my friend from the Gulf War, Dave Scarano. All told I finished the ride 7 times over the years.

"Diesel Dave crosses the finish line, Mt Mitchell, 1992"

Another similar challenging ride was the Bridge to Bridge Incredible Challenge. This ride originally started in Hickory, NC and finished at the summit of Grandfather Mountain. After the first few years the starting point was moved to Lenoir, NC, but with both routes, the distance remained the same, *"101 Miles of Pure Hill"* as the ride was advertised.

As best as I can remember this event was held for the first time in the early 1990s and I participated a total of 6 times over the years. This ride was unique in that the first 50 miles were rather tame, except for one or two steep climbs. But at the 50-mile point we made a right turn onto Highway 181 and began climbing. For… twelve… solid…miles! It was brutal. When we made it to the top of that climb, we entered the Blue Ridge Parkway. There we did some more climbs, mixed with some nice descents. It was surely more uphill than down. And as our bike computers turned over to 99 miles, we made a right turn into the Grandfather Mountain Park. It was there that we were greeted with a sign that said, "2 miles to the summit". Heck, only two more miles?!! How hard could it be?

"Diesel Dave (white helmet) and Mike Haney (yellow

helmet) making their way up the final climb, Grandfather Mountain, 2005"

The last two miles would take many of us almost an hour to complete. It was brutal; in our lowest gears we could barely turn the pedals. We were constantly stopping to rest. About halfway up this final climb we could look up and see the switchbacks that would take us to the top. What we also saw, as I like to describe it, was total carnage! Cyclists were laying in the road, groaning with leg cramps, or walking their bikes, or just sitting there waiting for a SAG wagon to pick them up! There was a small cut-out on the side of the road that Mike Haney and I would stop for a rest. Mike and I were equal in skill and normally did the entire ride together. I would ask, "Tell me again, Mike, why are we doing this?" And he would reply "Because there is beer at the top!" Somehow, we put our minds to the task, sucked up the pain, and always managed to make it to the top on our bikes. Thankfully, there were people at the finish line who would catch us before we fell over.

"Front row, l to r, Diesel Dave, Mike Haney, Keith Hines. Back row Nick Galloway, Jared Hand, Chuck Hand, Neal Price - Grandfather Mountain, 2006"

This fantastic ride met its demise several years ago, I don't really know why because it was always well attended. But many of our Seyboros had the opportunity to ride it at least one time over the years. Often people would ask me, "Which ride is tougher, Mitchell or Bridge to Bridge?" My answer would be, "I can't really tell you." Realistically, I think my answer depended on which ride I had done more recently and was fresher in my memory.

"The final climb to the top of Grandfather Mountain"

Lots of funny things happened on our trips to both of these mountain rides. One of the more memorable involves my good friend Jörg's ride on Bridge to Bridge. I've got to tell you, Jörg is a big man, about 6'4", 250 pounds. He was perhaps the fastest sprinter in our club. But his size was a detriment to climbing hills; he was carrying a lot of weight up those mountains. He didn't want to do the ride, but a bunch of us bugged and challenged him until he finally said "yes". There were probably eight of us doing the ride that year. Following the start, none of us ever saw Jörg again. We all finished the ride, between 6 and 8 hours, and were waiting at the top on news about Jörg.

There are time limits for the Bridge to Bridge ride. All cyclists must enter the Grandfather Mountain Park by 5pm (9 hours after the start time). Jörg tells us shortly after he entered the park, he heard the distinctive sound of metal on metal, as the attendant closed the gate. He figured "Well, I might be the last one on the route, but I'm gonna finish". A few moments later he realized that one more man had entered the park behind him before the gate was closed. The man slowly rode past Jörg, and he was astonished to see the man only had one leg! That's right. Our club's fastest sprinter was beaten to the top of Grandfather Mountain by a one-legged man! You'd better believe, Jörg has never heard the end of this story!

Years later, Bryan Ream joined our club and before long he had developed into one of our strongest riders. He decided to add his name to the Seyboro list of Bridge to Bridge finishers. As with many cyclists who've never done a mountain ride, Bryan found the ride to be extremely tough. But he persisted. It took him a long time, but he finally made it to the entrance, with just 2 miles to go. Halfway up, he found the same picnic table that Mike Haney and I often rested at. Bryan stretched out on top of the table for a brief nap, before finishing the last mile. The next thing Bryan knew, the park ranger was waking him up and telling him the park was closed, he needed to get off the mountain. Needless to say, Bryan caught a lot of flak about his "DNF"! He had to wait a year to avenge his mishap. He returned the next year later to conquer the Grandfather and did so in good time.

Over the years, hundreds of Seyboro jerseys have been seen on the mountain roads of western North Carolina. On the rides up Grandfather and My Mitchell, which normally see an average of 25% or more non-finishers, our club's completion rate is better than 95%. I like to think this has a lot to do with the grit and determination of our club members. Anytime a new person joins our group, everybody has jumped in to help the new rider become strong and successful. We may be "flatlanders", but when the time comes to head uphill, we've always done well and held our heads high!

A Seyboro Memory

Frank had a friend, Randy, who lived in Wilmington, and they'd both signed up to do the Assault on Mount Mitchell in the mid-1980s. They were friends, but fierce competitors. Both had the goal of beating the other to the top. They rode together for the first 70 miles.

As they approached Marion, Randy complained about not feeling well. Frank encouraged Randy to stop at a McDonald's restaurant ahead, and eat a couple of Big Macs. Randy followed Frank's advice as Frank rode ahead with a smirk on his face. 20 minutes later Randy was back on his bike. He made it about 3 miles up the climb to the Parkway when he pulled off the side of the road, and fell into the ditch, vomiting.

Along came one of the bicycle magazine writers, who photo'd Randy curled up in a ball, laying in the ditch. The photo made it into the magazine with a quote from Randy, *"I'm gonna lay right here until my wife picks me up."* Frank went ahead and finished the ride, giving him bragging rights over Randy.

Chapter 7
Tour de Fools

How do you define a fool? According to Webster's dictionary, a person lacking in judgment or prudence is a fool. Whereas, according to Seyboro dictionary, cyclists who do crazy things are fools.

By this time, you must be thinking that our worlds revolved around cycling, which would not be wrong to say. Our lives did revolve around it, and we were always looking for new ways to make riding bicycles enjoyable. Many years ago, one of our club members came up with an idea of doing a multi-day ride, making it open to all the club members interested in taking part. I don't know who came up with the name 'Tour de Fools,' but the rides have certainly lived up to the moniker.

In all these years of learning and growing together, Seyboros learned that our road trips were a heck of a lot of fun ever since the inception of the Mount Mitchell rides. From the time we were on the bikes, to time off bicycles that we spent together, joking around and pranking with each other, telling stories, sharing experiences, and just spending time with terrific friends that we had become - it was all so much fun. We had just as much fun off the bikes as we did while riding.

The Blue Ridge Parkway Ride

Approximately 20 years ago, a few of our club members came up with the whacky idea of doing a 5-day ride on the Blue Ridge Parkway. The group members included Jörg Wagner, Pat Hawkins, Tom Bradshaw, and Dana Rice. They planned the ride with a few of Tom's relatives, including his brother Richard. They also invited a lot of the Seyboros, perhaps the rest of us were smarter than them and said, *"No!"*

The Blue Ridge is a beautiful ride… on a motorcycle! What were these guys thinking? Anyone in their right senses would know that it is going to be one hell of a ride. There are no flat surfaces on the parkway, you are either going uphill or downhill; no matter in which direction you ride, there seems to be about 90% up and only 10% down. The group quickly found out that the 'group' ride was not going to happen. Whenever cyclists ride in the mountains, their varying skills come into play, and they rarely stay together. Normally the lean riders without much weight can climb better than the stocky folks. It is obvious that when you are heavier, it takes time to push yourself up to a mountain. However, the same heavy riders will often catch the lighter ones on the way down the hill because of gravity. Nevertheless, from what I hear, the original 'Tour de Fools' was fun, but most of the riders spent their days riding by themselves.

The North Carolina Coast Ride

Several years later, the Seyboros came up with another new idea for a ride; we decided to ride the North Carolina coast. In this 'Tour de Fools', we left Goldsboro on the first day and rode a hundred miles south to Wilmington. The next day took us from Wilmington, following the coast roads, to Morehead City, about 90 miles. On day three, we rode north up the coastline to Cedar Island. The road ends there, and we had to take a ferry boat ride of about two hours to the island of Ocracoke since none of us was an outstanding swimmer. Once we were on the island, we rode about 15 miles from south to north. It was a pretty exciting ride, for it included activities other than just cycling. The island was charming. It was so narrow we could see the ocean on both sides. When we arrived at our northern destination, we boarded on another ferry boat to ride to the mainland at Hatteras. Both the ferry rides were fun and refreshing. We got a chance to relax from the constant pedaling in the scorching summer heat. When we arrived at Hatteras, we pedaled a few miles to our hotel for that night. The third day was one of our shortest days, only about 70 miles.

On the fourth day, we rode from Hatteras north to Kill Devil Hills. Something strange happened that day. While we were heading north on Highway 12, a truck filled with construction workers passed by, they yelled obscenities at us, telling us to get off their f***ing roads. This was not the Hatteras Tourist Welcoming committee, and it is pretty apparent that we responded with some inappropriate gestures. Within 10 minutes, all seven of us were standing on the highway's shoulder, fixing flat tires.

There stood Chuck Hand, Scott Summers, Jörg Wagner, Mike Haney, Dan Olsen, Steve '21' Desrochers, and me, all within 100 yards of each other, replacing the tubes on the front or rear tire of our bikes. We noticed an unusual amount of roofing nails had been thrown all along the shoulder of the road. It appeared that the 'welcoming committee' had gotten the last laugh. Thankfully we had a SAG vehicle with us, several of our wives were driving. We went through a lot of inner tubes that day.

We finished up that day's ride at our hotel in Kill Devil Hills with about 75 miles in total. Jörg was not satisfied, though. He insisted that we should ride up to Corolla, on the northern edge of the Outer Banks, for this to be a 'true' Tour de fools. He got several fools to agree with him, and we took off for another 40 miles or more. We ran into some heavy traffic, and we were already exhausted from four days of riding in the heat and humidity, so it was some tough going.

When we returned to the hotel, we found the other guys lounging by the pool with some cold drinks. We accused them of not being 'true finishers' of the tour and argued with them, good-naturedly of course, well into the evening. To this day, the argument goes on as to who rode the 'entire' Tour de Fools that year.

On day five, we woke up early and rode about 60 miles inland to the town of Elizabeth City and completed the ride all by eating the most giant burger Hardees had on their menu. We had earned it. We rode a little more than 400 miles in five days, which was also in the high heat and humidity of summer in North Carolina. We had also battled some heavy winds at times, as the ocean breezes are always rather formidable, but we made it through it all. Another fun, crazy Seyboro ride was under our belts with lots of fun, fights, stupid moments, and memories.

The Natchez Trace Ride

Several years later, we came up with the idea of riding the Natchez Trace. This is a federal parkway that runs between Natchez, Mississippi and Nashville, Tennessee. It's a total of 440 miles in length and takes in parts of Mississippi, Alabama, and Tennessee. A beautiful ride on a bicycle, indeed. Jörg, Chuck Hand, Mike Haney, Kyle Robinson, Bobby Baker, and I decided to make the trip. It takes a lot of work and pre-planning to do a ride of this magnitude. We'd rent a large van and stay at B&Bs along the way. Chuck's wife, Velvie, and Kyle's wife, Maureen, volunteered to drive the van for us each day. We planned to ride about 90 miles per day.

Not all the B&Bs were 5-star!

The Beginning

On the first morning, we went to Denny's restaurant's all you can eat for breakfast. Bobby was our roast-target that day. We teased him a lot, telling him we didn't know when we would be able to eat again, so he'd better eat up. We kept sending him back to get more food. He ate so much that he was vomiting before we ever got on our bikes. That's the kind of prank that our club has been famous for.

We got on the road at about 9 AM and headed north. Chuck kept insisting we would see a lot of armadillos. We told him he was crazy; there weren't any armadillos in that area. Chuck, of course, went crazy. When we finally saw one, Chuck shouted, "See!! I told you, I told you." We all insisted he'd seen a squirrel, and we stuck together. When we stopped at a quick-mart in a small town for more water, Chuck ran around to all the locals in the store, saying, *"Hey, don't you have a lot of armadillos around here?"* The folks were looking at Chuck like he might be a little bit crazy, and behind his back, we were sort of acknowledging that they were right.

Chuck did get some revenge on me, though. A little bit later, when we were back on the road, I got stung by a wasp on the bridge of my nose. *"Somebody give me a credit card or driver's license,"* Chuck yelled. Somebody produced a card, and Chuck commenced to start scraping the bridge of my nose, declaring he needed to remove the stinger, and did he ever scrape. I believe he got all the way down to the bone. I forgot all about the bee sting; now I had blood running down my face, yet another case of unruly Seyboro behavior.

The ladies met us with the van about halfway every day, and we would find a nice, shady place along the road for lunch. The ladies spoiled us for sure; they went out of their way to prepare some great sandwiches and snacks. We feasted well at lunch and then ate well again each evening. A beautiful thing about riding a bike 90 miles a day is that you don't have to worry too much about counting calories.

The route was beautiful the entire way. The first two days were supposed to be rather flat terrain. On the afternoon of the second day, though, we looked ahead at one point and saw a monstrous hill rising in front of us. We knew there were some big hills on the route but weren't expecting them until day three. We all had 'flatland' gears on our bikes and struggled to make it up that hill. That evening we ate dinner, drank beer, and changed the rear cogs on our bikes with lower gears. Day three was challenging, and the last two days threw some more hills at us.

The parkway had mile markers, so we agreed that we would take turns pulling for a mile, then drop back and sit in the draft. We'd use the mile markers as our cue to drop off. This way, we'd only pull once every 6 miles. I could swear the other guys went out each night, removed every 6th-mile marker, and arranged for me to ride two miles every time I pulled. It seemed that way, anyhow. Can't trust those Seyboros!

The entire trip was a blast. The weather was perfect, and despite being attacked continuously by armadillos, we made it to the finishing parking lot on the afternoon of our fifth day. Jörg astutely noticed that we weren't really at the end of the Natchez Trace Parkway. The parking lot was located about a half-mile inside of the parkway. Hence, as all the others pulled into the parking lot, whooping and hollering, Jörg and I kept riding. We rode to the sign indicating the start/finish of the parkway, Jörg snapped a photo, and we returned to the parking lot.

When we got back on the road for our return trip back home, we announced to the others that, unfortunately, they couldn't take credit for 'finishing' the ride. *"What are you talkin' about?"* asked Bobby. Jörg told them that only he and I rode all the way to the finishing point, and he had the photo to prove it. In true Seyboro fashion, this created an argument that lasted about half the way home.

The end? No. The beginning

It was never an end for us passionate cyclists; every ride that we finished was just the beginning of another one. We have held about five more 'Tour de Fools' over the years, all of them riding on the Great Allegheny Passage (Gap) and C&O Canal. The GAP runs from Pittsburg, PA to Cumberland, MD, which is about 140 miles in length, on old converted railroad beds. The C&O Canal is about 180 miles and picks up at the finish of the GAP. The canal towpath continues the trip to Georgetown, near Washington D.C.

Cyclists can ride all or parts of these two routes. They have been convenient for our club to reach the starting point in a day's drive. Neither course is paved; the surface is anything from dirt (muddy!) pathway to packed, crushed limestone. Only hikers and bicyclists are allowed on the routes. The lack of vehicular traffic certainly makes us feel safer as we ride.

On these tours, we would take anywhere between 3 to 5 days, depending on how far we were planning to ride. We weren't on asphalt and were riding hybrid or mountain bikes, and usually made it 50 to 60 miles a day. We stayed in motels at night. A few times, we discussed camping, but after a long bike ride in the heat, we all decided we would rather have air-conditioned rooms and hot showers in the evenings. The best part about these tours; the evenings were as much a part of the fun as the rides. We would sit around and drink a few beers and talk about the day's events. We talked a lot of smack and joked around with each other.

I am trying my best to remember all our club members who participated in these rides. Frank Drohan, Tom Bradshaw, Steve 21, Mike Haney, Joe Austin, Dan Mayette, and I have ridden all or several. We have also had Joe's wife, Pat Austin, Frank's son Paul, Kat McGhee, and David Neirenburg along for at least one of the trips. What a blast we've had, and I could probably fill up an entire book with stories about the rides.

A tour by the 'Three'

I can remember one particular tour that sticks out in my mind. Five years ago, we did a tour that only included three members from our club; Mike, Frank, and me. We started in Pittsburg and hoped to make it to D.C. My wife Kay stayed in Cumberland to visit her sister, Mary. We'd hoped to make it to Cumberland in two days, but I developed some physical problems with my back on day two. Kay and Mary picked me up near Meyersdale, PA, and drove me to Cumberland while Frank and Mike finished the ride there.

We spent the night in Cumberland, and it rained all night. The next day our destination was Hancock, Maryland, about 50 miles. My back felt a little better, so the three of us set out early in the morning. We were now on the C&O Canal, and the path was no more than a dirt road leaving out of Cumberland, so we were slogging through 3 inches or more of mud a lot of the way, tough going. Kay and Mary had offered to drive Sag, and they met us in Spring Gap about 10 miles east of Cumberland. We discussed the mud and the difficult travel, but none of us wanted to give up.

We told the ladies to meet us at the little store in PawPaw, West Virginia, for our next stop. A passer-by had told us PawPaw was only about 10 miles, so we told the ladies we would be there in about an hour. We didn't realize that the passer-by was laughing his butt off as he rode away or was poorly informed. We headed out of Spring Gap and hit even worse mud than we had been riding through. We were barely doing 5 or 6 mph, and we rode and rode and rode.

I haven't discussed my accident much, for I am leaving that story for another book. To suffice, I had been in a bad bicycling accident in 2006. Ever since that time, Kay would be very nervous every time I am out on the bike. She had received that call on the fateful day of my accident and arrived at the hospital to find me clinging to life. So, whenever I was on the bike and didn't show up at the time she expected me to, she began to panic and expected the worse. We rode for two hours straight and had no idea how much longer it would take. Therefore, we stopped and tried to call Kay. You have got to realize; we were in the mountains of West Virginia, which means no cellphone signals at all. Three different phones, three different cell companies, zero services on any. We had no choice but to keep riding. As we approached the PawPaw tunnel, we knew we were finally getting close, but it had been almost three hours since we saw the ladies. Still no cellphone service. Kay was frantic by now.

The PawPaw Tunnel

The PawPaw tunnel is really neat. It's over half a mile long and has a narrow, rugged walkway on one side with the canal running through the middle of the tunnel. A slip could put you over the railing and into the water. For some reason, though, I couldn't figure out what, when we arrived at the tunnel, something didn't seem right. I had been through it several times. We went on through the tunnel, rode part of the way, and sometimes had to walk our bikes. Headlights were essential. It was so dark in the middle of the tunnel that both ends looked the size of a pinhead. When we came out on the other side, I told Mike and Frank that something was not right. We tried our phones, still no luck. About that time, we saw two headlights coming towards us through the tunnel. We waited for them to exit. It was two young ladies, and as we talked to them, we realized we had ridden past the town of PawPaw before we had come to the tunnel. It turned out we had ridden right past Kay and Mary; the store where they were waiting could not be seen from the bike's path. I was having strange feelings because I did not realize that when we approached the tunnel, we had already passed the small town of PawPaw.

By now, I was frantic too because I knew Kay would be panicking. Mike and Frank said they would go on to the store; they could get there much faster than me. We needed to go back through the tunnel, and I did not trust myself riding the bike; I decided I would walk it. So, they took off for PawPaw and left me to follow. I was having a hard time, even to move by now. My back was acting up again, and I have never walked well since my accident. It took me a long time to get through the tunnel. Mike and Frank arrived at the store. Kay and Mary were so relieved to see them but asked where I was. They explained I would be along shortly. Kay was not happy about that and told Mary she should get in the car and find me.

Mike and Frank had parked their bikes and headed into the store for a cold drink. As Mike was coming out of the store, a man stopped him and said, *"Hey Mister, some lady just ran over your bike."* Mike looked, and sure enough, Mary had run over his bike on her way out of the parking lot to look for me. She drove about a half-mile and found me coming towards her on my bike, so she turned around and returned to the store; I arrived a moment later.

I am not sure if Kay was extremely mad or delighted to see me. She had been so worried. Our one-hour estimated time had turned into more than 3 hours. After two hours, she had started making phone calls. She called the National Park Police, along with both the West Virginia and Maryland State Police agencies. There was not much any of them could do, but the Maryland trooper asked Kay for a description. Instead of saying, *"Three old men wearing Lycra and riding mountain bikes,"* she said, *"My husband is on a gray bike with a black bag on the handlebars with a handgun in it."*

What was she even thinking!?? Maryland doesn't play nice when it comes to guns; they are one of the most anti-gun states in the country. While I hold a concealed carry permit in North Carolina, Maryland doesn't recognize any out-of-state licenses. When Kay narrated this story to us, we decided our best bet was to load the bikes into the car, head for Hancock, and call it a day before the state police showed up. Mike's front wheel was trashed, so he couldn't have ridden anyhow. They may still have an outstanding warrant for me in Maryland.

The next morning my back was still bad, so I lent Mike my front wheel. He and Frank continued the tour towards Harper's Ferry, while I rode in the vehicle with Mary and Kay. I continued to get a tongue lashing from Kay for the previous day. It wasn't like we planned things to go the way they did, and it wasn't like we didn't try to call her. Like Forrest Gump said, *"Sometimes shit happens!"*

We wrapped up our Tour de 'Fools that evening without making it to Georgetown. We had no regrets. For sure, we had a fun time and lots of memories to relive. I still tease Kay about the time she tried to get me locked up in jail. All of our tours on the GAP and C&O Canal are memorable, and we plan more in the future for sure.

As I said earlier, the end of every ride is the beginning of another, so as I write this book, we are planning to do a ride again this year, but the COVID-19 might change our plans. Anyway, whenever we make the trip, we are sure it will create more funny and memorable moments than ever. The camaraderie just can't be beaten.

The rides we have had, all of them are very dear to me, but I close this chapter with a bit of sadness in my heart. I can't think of our rides on the Gap and C&O canal without remembering two of our fallen riders, Tom Bradshaw and Joe Austin. They both loved these rides, and we loved having them with us. They both passed away in 2019, and our tours won't be the same without them. Nonetheless, I am sure they both are sitting together in heaven, looking down on us, and saying, *"Keep the rides going, Seyboros. Our spirits are with you!"*

A Seyboro Memory

On our Tour de Fools ride of the North Carolina coastline, myself, Steve 21 and Scott Summers encountered a problem at our hotel on the third night. We'd reserved a room for the three of us. When we checked in, we found the room had two double beds, and the hotel was out of roll-away beds. So now we were three guys, and two bed; somebody was going to have to share a bed. Scott came up with the idea, let's do 'Rock, Paper, Scissors.' The winner would get a bed to himself.

We proceeded to start. In the first game, we all three did 'rock.' Nobody won. The second time, we all did 'paper.' Again, no winner. We tried a third time, and this time we all did 'rock' again.

Steve 21 settled things. Obviously, there was no winner. All three of us slept in the same bed that night....

Chapter 8
The Double Century

As if 100 miles on a bicycle weren't enough!

Cycling is an addiction; once you start cycling, there is no looking back. You ride for hours and cover miles, and yet you feel it is not enough. You feel like you are being challenged by the invisible forces to cover up distance more than you had earlier. You are so crazy that you are even willing to travel around the world to participate in a ride, just like I did in 2002. I traveled to South Carolina, for I had been invited to join one of their bike rides. My son, Nick, and my friend, Jörg accompanied me.

When we arrived, we found a group of friendly cyclists, including both men and women. They were in the middle of the process of attempting a double century. When we arrived, they had just completed the first 50-miles as part of the ride, whereas we joined them for the remaining three loops of the ride. They planned to ride four different 50-mile loops, all in one day with a hope to finish before sunset.

For those who are still not aware of what I mean when I say double century, it means 200 miles ridden in one day. You may as well wonder why on earth anyone would want to ride 200 miles a day. I would say it's just another challenge that elite cyclists aspire to take. Call us crazy; maybe we are! Especially when it comes to riding a bicycle, there is nothing in this world that can stop us. I have met many accomplished and strong cyclists who have been riding for many years, never having a desire to take on such crazy endeavors, and I cannot blame them. For many of us, though, it's just another challenge.

It would not be wrong to say that our friends in South Carolina were successful, some of them, at least. When we joined them at 50, there were about a dozen other riders beside us. By the end of the day, only five of the South Carolina guys were still going; the rest had dropped out at various points of the day. The five finishers were extremely proud as they should have been. It sure was an accomplishment. Even Jörg, Nick, and I were proud of ourselves, for none of us had ridden 150 miles in one day.

The first Seyboro Double Century Ride

On our way back to Goldsboro, our plan was hatched. We were excited about what we had done and figured the crazy Seyboros would love such a crazy idea of a 200-miles ride. We began making plans for the first Seyboro Cyclist double century to be held in 2003. We picked mid-June for the ride because that's when we have the most sunlight. We hoped to start at 6 AM and finish by sunset, devising a plan similar to the one our friends in South Carolina used but with altered mileage of different routes. We figured to start with a 65-mile loop, followed by 55 miles, 45 miles, and 35 miles. This way, it would be easier for the riders to finish the ride and stay motivated.

There was a method to our madness. Long-distance cycling can often be as much of a mental challenge as a physical one. *"Can I do this?"* or *"Will I be able to finish?"* These were the kind of questions that arose in our heads. We had more than a hundred club members at the time, and half of them were willing to go for a double century ride. They had all ridden at least one century in their cycling career. Could they ride two? Well, it was just a matter of time.

The route

By reducing the length of each section of the ride, we hoped to give a mental edge to those who could finish the first two loops. This way, they would not just give in thinking that it's just a few more miles. The plan was to ride a 65-mile loop starting at the Eastern Wayne High School in Goldsboro. The route would go northwest, using a major part of our Harvest Hundred route.

We would then return to the school where we would have our cars parked and stocked with ice chests, cold drinks, snacks, cookies, and lots of other foods loaded with carbohydrates. We would take a 15-minutes break to eat, drink, elevate our legs, or do whatever we needed to do to relax.

After the break, we would be on the road again, and this time, for 55 miles. The second loop would take us northeast to the small town of Hookerton and back to the school. The riders would have 120 miles under their belts, well over halfway to the goal. By this time, we knew that a lot of fatigue would be setting in. After we had our break, we would be looking at a 45-mile ride, a pretty normal ride for our club, followed by another break. At that point, the riders would have completed 165 miles. How could they give up now? Heck, we sometimes did a 35 miles ride just to warm up! (Now you do know that I am exaggerating a little bit!) But to tell the truth, our hard-core group of Seyboro Cyclists would regularly ride 35 miles for our evening rides, and we would still finish full of spit and vinegar! Therefore, 35 miles would hopefully appear doable at this point in the day.

Set of Rules

We had set several rules for the participants; one was to maintain a speed of 18 mph. Not more, not less. It would allow us to complete the ride, even with breaks, and before the sunset. Folks who could not hold the pace would be left on their own, but we would try to have a SAG vehicle available to pick them up. We did not mean to sound insensitive, but we could not let one person's failure jeopardize everybody else's chance at finishing.

We would only stop for minor mechanical issues such as a flat tire. Those of us with lots of experience can fix a flat in an instant and be back on the road within 5 minutes. But in case of any significant malfunctions, we would leave them to the SAG vehicle. Folks were only invited to come out and ride as many loops as they want, they could back out after one or two. Riding the entire 200 miles was up to each individual's capability.

Our biggest concern was dealing with a few hammerheads who show up for one or two loops, getting up the front of the group, and pushing the speed up to 20 or more mph. While most of us were able to hold a speed of 20mph or more, we had never dared to try doing it for a 200 miles ride, which was not the time to try.

Therefore, to prevent this from happening, about five club leaders memorized the routes and kept them in our heads. We did not hand out maps, so if somebody decided to show us how strong they were by picking up the pace, we would just let them go. They wouldn't go far, as they will not have a map! We were just praying that at least one of us leaders would be able to hang in for the entire ride.

The Beginning of the ride; Loop-1

The day of our first double century arrived in June of 2003. We had advertised the ride in eastern North Carolina and had a huge turnout. Besides the Seyboros, the groups that showed up were from Wilson, Jacksonville,

Fayetteville, and Raleigh. All the rules had been well-publicized.

Some folks told us upfront that they were not going to ride the entire 200 miles, which was fine. The more riders we had, the more help we would have with taking pulls at the front of the group, cutting through the wind to aid the rest of us. At 6 AM, we all gathered near New Hope Road, took some photos, and somebody led us in prayer. Then we were off.

Thankfully it was the early morning of a Saturday, so the traffic was at a minimum; our group was riding double file and stretched out for quite some distance. My mind was racing, for I had been one of the driving forces behind this madness! Would I be able to finish?

At this point, I had been riding for almost 20 years and had plenty of experience. My yearly bike mileage averaged around 5,000 miles. I had also done some amateur racing and climbed the tallest mountains several times. Therefore, I knew that if I was ever going to be ready to ride a double century, it was now!

Our group was so large that sitting in the middle, doing 18 mph, did not seem difficult. The large group sort of just pulled me along. Of course, I took plenty of turns at the front too. Our first loop seemed to go by rather easily. We had planned a quick stop near Smithfield to refill our bottles, and we made it back to the school before 10 AM. So far, so good.

Loop-2

So far, the ride was going very smoothly. Some of our newest club members threw in the towel, but they had completed their first metric century by riding the first loop with us; it was a personal goal for them. At the same time, a few other new riders joined us for the second loop. In short, the loops were always open for participants to leave and join whenever they wanted.

We headed northeast for loop-2 shortly after 10 AM. The crowd was almost as large as the first group; therefore, we still had plenty of riders to share the work up at the front of the pack. A few riders were starting to fade, and we encouraged them just to sit in the middle or back of the peloton, and take advantage of the draft. We hit the halfway point, stopped at a store again for refills of water, and headed back.

However, we were now fighting a fairly strong headwind. This is where the going got tough! We were approaching 100 miles in the saddle, and fatigue was setting in. Then we hit highway 903, going south out of Snow Hill, and we also encountered some rolling hills. We powered on but began to lose some riders. They understood. The rules had been made clear in advance.

Most of those who dropped off did not need SAG support. They just told us to go on ahead; they would slow down and eventually make their way back to the school. We hated to ride away from them but still had a good-sized group of riders who were all hoping to complete the two hundred miles.

We rolled back into the school at about 1:30 in the afternoon. A few of us grabbed a quick shower in the school gym and put on clean and dry clothing. What a great feeling it was after a long ride! Others just fell out at their vehicles to rest and eat. Quite a few announced that they no longer had any desire to ride 200 miles in one day! *"What do you mean?"* the rest of us asked. But the ones who were abandoning had their minds made up. The heat, humidity, and fatigue were just too much to handle, they said. Most of them had never ridden for more than a century, so they had already set a new record. Try as we might, there was no changing their minds.

Loop-3

After an extended break, about 15 participants headed out for loop three at 2 PM. This route would take us north-northeast towards the small town of Stantonsburg. We were in the midst of the day's heat, and it was tough going. However, those of us still riding were now on a mission. If we could finish this loop, we would only be 35 miles away from our goal.

If I talk about myself, I was still feeling strong. I was eating and drinking right and taking reasonable pulls at the front. Keeping well hydrated was so crucial at this point, and I kept telling myself to drink frequently. We stopped at a store in Stantonsburg, which turned out to be a mistake for two of the riders. They got inside that air-conditioned store and said, *"I'm done. I'll try again next year!"*

We reluctantly left the air-conditioned store to head back to the school. At this point, things were relatively quiet in our peloton. We were all lost in our thoughts; will I finish the ride? I am still 50 miles from being done. I am hot, tired, sweaty, and just want to lie down for a nap! These were the thoughts going through all our minds. But we pressed on.

Still in the peloton with me were Seyboros Scott Summers, Sarah Alholm, Chuck Hand, Mike Haney, Calvin Ford, and Mark Shroyer. We still had about five of our friends from Fayetteville, including Furman, who was probably the strongest in the entire group. The club from Fayetteville included two ladies, and they were riding just as vigorously as the men. Ed Frantz and another man from Raleigh were also still with us. The last 20 miles of the third leg was probably the quietest ones of the day. We were downright worn-out.

We rolled into the school's parking lot at 4:45 PM. Our vehicles sure looked tempting. We had ridden 165 miles, a personal best for everyone except Furman. Could we talk ourselves into doing 35 more miles? Most of us did. We lost a few of our visiting riders. They just felt they could not go on. The rest decided to extend our break at the school by just a few minutes and then depart for the last leg.

Loop-4; The Final Loop

A boost to our morale came in the form of a few fresh riders from our Seyboro club. They had not ridden with us yet that day but showed up for the final loop. They had figured we could use some extra muscle on the last loop, and they were right! They were a sight for sore eyes. It was nice to know we had some fresh legs and lungs to take some of the pulls at the front of the group, let us sit in a little bit more.

At 5:15, we headed out for our last leg of the trip. We were getting pumped up now! The end was in sight. Even though we had lost a few riders, we'd picked up some new ones, so we probably had about 15 participants. We continued to power along at 18 mph. I have been known to holler, *"I feel good"* at the top of my lungs, even when I don't feel good, but I was hollering a lot in the last section. We had a SAG wagon with us, driven by a few of our lady members, and they would hand us a cold Gatorade out the window when we asked.

About halfway through that last leg, the group woke up and began to get a little frisky! We knew now that we would finish, and we were all filled with a new sense of excitement and strength. The speed started to pick up a little, and everyone hung on. We hit New Hope Road, riding west, and knew we were only 3 miles from the school. Most of our computers were reading 198 miles, and got us all laughing, *"Hey, what's going on? You mean we have got to ride the extra mile? The 200 miles isn't enough?"*

We were certainly euphoric at this point in the ride! Several of us were frisky enough even to try sprinting to be the first one done. I cannot remember who it was, but it was not me. At just about 7:15 PM, we all pulled into the school parking lot, dismounted our bikes, and began a 'hug-fest' that lasted for 5 minutes.

We gathered for some photos and shared a few drinks. Somebody had some beer on ice. About 10 of us had finished our double century, two hundred miles on a bicycle in one day. The next time you make a similar trip in your car, think about that. How can a person ride a bicycle that far? I say it's through sheer grit, the determination will power, and I give some of the credit to God, who gives me the strength and mental power required to do it. We sat around for about 15 minutes or so and reveled our accomplishment. I don't know this for a fact, but I would be willing to bet that less than one percent of the cycling community ever achieves such a goal.

The Last Laugh of the Day

We got our last laugh of the day as we watched Mark Shroyer. He stood up from his seat on the back of somebody's SUV and began walking to his car. He looked so pathetic! He could barely walk and kept stopping as he was overcome with leg cramps. We joked with him; he needed one of us to get his car for him; it was only about 50 yards away. He used his last little burst of energy to raise his middle finger to us. A fitting Seyboro goodbye!

Our double centuries turned into a yearly event for the Seyboro Cyclists for many years. In 2006, I finished my 4th in a row and held the club record for completions. I was matched by our friend Furman from Fayetteville, who had also finished all four. My double century days would come to an end in six months when I was involved in a terrible accident. Read about that in my sequel to this book.

But the double century tradition continued for quite a few years. I've compiled a list of finishers that appears at the end of this chapter. And the club is just crazy enough that they may try again in a future year.

In the past, Chuck Hand and his wife Velvie made things even more pleasurable when they would offer up a hot tub party at their house following the ride. I remember how good that hot tub felt on my tired body after such a long ride! Just another example of the type of folks we have in our club! Thanks, Chuck and Velvie!

I am so proud of our club! I think if you asked any one of these finishers what gave them the desire and ability to accomplish such a feat, they would put the credit on the Seyboro Cyclists club, and the way we ride, train and encourage each other, at the same time, we have a lot of fun too!

The Record-Breaking Vomit

On one of our early double centuries, Steve 21 was hanging tough well into the 3rd loop. We were approaching 150 miles and coming into the small town of La Grange. I looked over at Steve as he dropped off the front, and he had a pained look on his face. I asked him if he was feeling OK, and he said no, he had an upset stomach. We decided to take a quick stop at a small store to refill our bottles. There were probably about 20 riders in our group. We parked our bikes out front, leaning them up against the windows and went into the store. A minute later, one of our riders came running into the store and said, *"Hey, y'all need to come and check out Steve!"* *"What's wrong?"* we asked. *"Just come out here, you'll see!"*

We all departed the store and followed the guy around to the side of the building. Steve was sitting up against the side of the building, projecting vomit about a good 10 feet or more in front of him. He'd sit for maybe 5 or 10 seconds and do it all over again. We didn't know if we should cheer for him or feel sorry for him, so we all started clapping! We'd never seen anyone vomit like that! He had to be setting some sort of a world record. We thought about calling the EPA, having them come in and set up a hazard zone, perhaps evacuate all families within a mile.

It turns out that Steve was experiencing a medical condition called hyponatremia. It is a condition that can develop if someone drinks too much water while exercising.

Steve had been bragging about wearing his camelback, a water bladder that athletes can wear on their backs. He had taken in way too much water during the ride.

After having a lot of fun at Steve's expense, and making sure he was really OK, we called the SAG wagon to come to pick him up. To this day, there is some discoloration on the concrete beside that store in La Grange. It's probably caused by some excessive rainwater running off the building, but we always tell our new club members the story about Steve 21 and swear that Steve's vomit caused the discoloration, many years ago.

At the end of the day, we were happy that we had set a new cycling milestone and looked forward to breaking more records other than just vomiting. There is no end to where we could go cycling.

Two hundred miles on a bike in one day - how much better could it get?!!

SEYBORO CYCLIST DOUBLE CENTURY FINISHERS

Adrian McLawhorn	Agatija McAllister	Aldo Palacios
Bryan Ream	*Calvin Ford	*Carole Stanton
Caroline Mutters	Catherine Hamilton	*Chuck Hand
Dave Carter	*Dave Galloway	Dave Guerra
Dave Nierenberg	*Dave Valenzuela	*Ed Frantz
Elissa Ballas	*Furman Hamonds	Heather Barbaro
*Jim Harry	Jörg Wagner	Kat McGee
Keith Hines	Lisa Mathias	Mark Shroyer
*Mary Florian	*Mike Haney	Mike Thomas
Sarah Alholm	*Scott Summers	Shawna Dane
Steve Watson	Terry Forrest	*Tom Florian

* Indicates multiple finishes

I suspect there are more! Please forgive me if I left your name out, it certainly isn't intentional. A double Century is a team effort, and all finishers played a part in making this ride a success.

A Seyboro Memory

Chuck Hand was one of our strongest riders. He was fiercely competitive but a real gentleman. He served in the Air Force as a fighter pilot and retired at the rank of Lieutenant Colonel. Both of his sons, Justin and Jared, had grown up with the same positive attributes as their dad. Both graduated from the Air Force Academy and served in the Air Force as pilots.

Chuck was one of our club members who had completed several of our double centuries. Finishers of this grueling ride held an elite reputation in the club. During our 2009 event, Chuck pulled off to the side of the road, fell over, and curled into a fetal position, screaming with painful leg cramps. We were only 20 miles from the finish, and in Chuck's mind, being a non-finisher was an unfathomable thought.

The rest of us sat around on our bikes, trying to encourage Chuck, but his screams only got louder. Suddenly, Justin, who had joined the ride during the last section to accompany his dad, began cussing at his dad with words that would make a sailor blush. We all had known Justin as a quiet and polite young man. To hear such language from him was truly unbelievable.

As the moments went by, it only got worse until suddenly, Chuck stopped moaning and sat up. *"Hey guys, somebody give me a hand getting back up,"* he said. We got him up, he climbed aboard his bike, and said, *"OK, let's get rolling."* To our surprise, Chuck went on to finish the double. We later found out that Chuck had given instructions to Justin, *"Don't let me quit! No matter what, do what you must, but don't let me quit!"* Justin surely did take his dad's advice to heart.

Chapter 9
The Bicycle Inn

"Nothing compares to the simple pleasure of a bike ride."

-*John F. Kennedy*

Many years ago, most probably around 1995, one of our club members discovered a quaint little Bed and Breakfast nestled in the heart of the Blue Ridge Mountains near the town of Bakersville, NC. I cannot really remember who discovered this place. It may have been Pat Hawkins, Ernie Marshall, or 'Guido.' Still, the Bicycle Inn started another new chapter in the history of the Seyboro Cyclists that has left us with many fond memories to cherish. We have many experiences linked to this one place. Some are funny, some are tragic, some are even scary, but at the end of the day, we could not help but fall in love with this place. It is also one of the reasons I have made it a separate chapter to focus entirely on the experiences of this beautiful and peaceful place.

The Perfect Getaway!

Our club members traveled to the Bicycle Inn around a half dozen times over the years because we absolutely adored it. The inn was in a house owned by Pauline Davis and her husband, Mike. They had spent countless hours, days, months, and years converting it from an old farmhouse into a beautiful Bed and Breakfast. The motif was 100% bicycling!

It had five available rooms. The double-occupancy rooms were named after famous cyclists, such as the Sean Kelly Room and the Eddie Merckx Room. They also had a room with bunk beds that could accommodate six or eight people; it was called the Peloton Room. This was the room where all the single guys would stay, and you can imagine the fun we would have in it. There was always a lot of cussing, fighting, bragging, arguing, and farting in this room. It was a two-story house with wrap-around porches. Pauline would cook the meals for us, and Mike would lead us on some bike rides. It was the perfect getaway! The weather in the mountains, even in the middle of the summer, was always ideal. I cannot remember if the rooms had air conditioning, or if they even needed it.

The temperatures on the porches were always ideal and soothing, even in the unbearable heat of the day. In fact, we would need to don a sweatshirt to keep the chill off our bodies in the evenings. I can tell you that many stories were told on those porches with lots of love, warmth, and bonding. Many friendships became deeper here.

The Bicycle Inn was about a five-hour drive from home, and we would convoy out there for our visits. We normally stayed there for three to five days. Groups as large as fifteen or as small as five made the trips. We were always warmly welcomed by Mike and Pauline and felt as if we were a part of their extended family.

As soon as we arrived, the cyclists among us would change into their riding gear for a ride led by Mike. He knew the area well and would ask, *"Do you want flat roads or mountains?"* or *"How far do you want to ride?"* He knew the area well and would always lead us on whatever type of route we were looking for. Our spouses would get settled into the rooms and then meet us on the porch to chat and enjoy some drinks. It was such a beautiful and peaceful getaway from our hectic lives. The environment there was so peaceful that we never wanted to go back home.

The Roan Moan Climb

One of our favorite routes was dubbed 'The Roan Moan' by Mike Davis. We rode it a bunch of times on our random visits. It was a metric century, 62 miles long, and included plenty of hills. It went to the top of Roan Mountain, a very steep 8-mile climb, and ended right on the border between North Carolina and Tennessee. From the top, we had a beautiful, curvy downhill ride almost all the way back to the Bicycle Inn.

We headed out one morning to climb the Roan Moan. Brenda Ormond was with us, and three miles into the ride, we started to climb up the Iron Mountain. This climb was steep, and probably three miles long. We spread out as normal on the climb and then regrouped back together at the top. After reaching the top, we started waiting for Brenda. It took her quite a while to reach the top. She dismounted her bike at the top and told us we were all crazy as hell.

She was through riding these hills and was going to get in the SAG vehicle. Our host at the Inn, Mike Davis, was driving the vehicle at the time. We tried to convince Brenda to keep riding, but she would not be deterred. She climbed into the vehicle with Mike, and the rest of us headed back out on our bikes. We rode about 40 more miles, and we were now approaching the base of Roan Mountain. We stopped at a store to stock up on more drinks and food before starting the climb we were all dreading. As we pulled out of the store, somebody looked down the road and said, *"Hey, here comes Brenda."* We all stopped and looked, and sure enough, we saw Brenda riding toward us or so we thought.

As she got closer, we recognized the white jersey, white helmet, and silver bike, but it appeared Brenda had a beard. As she got really close, we realized 'she' was actually Mike Davis. It turned out that when Brenda decided to ride in the SAG wagon, Mike had decided he would like to ride with us. He did not have a bike or the right clothing, so he switched clothes with Brenda and climbed aboard her bike after adjusting the seat. He looked somewhat silly, wearing a sleeveless women's jersey, but hey, he was riding, and that's what mattered at the time.

We headed out to the base of the mountain. One of our Seyboros, Calvin Ford, was making his debut visit to the Bicycle Inn. We had told Calvin about the Roan Moan but had played it down quite a bit. *"Oh, it's a little bit tough, but not so bad. Just a short climb."* Calvin was a strong rider, so we knew he could do the ride. But he sure did get angry with us when we started up the climb to the top of Roan Mountain!

What made the ride even more challenging were the mile markers on the way to the top. We would pass mile marker eight and ride for a long time until we'd see the mile marker 7. We would all get the feeling that we would never reach the top. We all climb mountains at a different pace, so we were spread out a lot on the climb. I remember climbing that mountain myself many times. I was an average climber, not the fastest or the slowest, but I was almost always by myself on the climb.

On this particular day, we could all hear Calvin hollering and cussing as we slowly made our way up the mountain. We couldn't see him, but sound travels and echoes well in the mountains. I was somewhere in front of Calvin on the climb. I heard him hollering, *"I'm gonna kill every one of you guys when I catch you,"* and *"I am gonna get my hands on a machine gun and mow every one of you down!"* I chuckled as I listened to him and thought, *"I may need to lock myself in my room when we get back, at least until Calvin settles down."*

When I reached the top, the guys in front of me had stopped to wait for the rest of the group, and we laughed as we listened to Calvin continuing to holler. About that time, Brenda showed up in the SAG vehicle and told us, *"Y'all need to get back down this mountain and stop Frank Drohan. He's having a hard time, and he's threatening to throw his bike over the side of the hill!"*

Obviously, Calvin was not the only one who was having trouble with Roan Mountain! A couple of us started back down the mountain and came across Frank within a quarter-mile. He was struggling, so we gave him some words of encouragement and some water, and he finally made it to the top. He was followed shortly by Calvin, who was so glad to finallyc reach the summit that he forgot all about killing or shooting us. When the entire group made it to the top, we started that long, graceful downhill ride back to the Inn, and you can believe there were a lot of stories told that night on the porch.

Pictures of the 'Birds' or 'Moon' maybe?

On one of our trips, Calvin had taken his camera. Remember, these were pre-cell phone days! He left his camera at the table on the porch and told us he was going to his room to shower. Brenda asked him before he left if it would be ok for her to take a few photos of the birds in the area, and Calvin replied, *"Sure!"* Calvin left to shower, Brenda left with the camera.

A few minutes later, Brenda returned with the camera and left it on the table. I am not sure who came up with the idea (certainly not me!) to have some of the guys 'moon' Calvin and snap some photos with his camera. The deed was done before he returned, and not a word was ever mentioned.

Several days later, we returned home. Calvin was anxious to see how his photos had turned out from the Bicycle Inn. He had snapped a couple of good action photos of us on our bikes. He took his film to the one-hour photo shop and waited for the photos to be developed. He was planning to have dinner with his Mom that night, so when the photos were developed and ready, he carried them to his Mom's house to share with her. He hadn't looked at them yet.

He arrived at this Mom's house. They sat down on her couch to view the photos of his cycling buddies. *"There's Pat and Susan Hawkins,"* he said. *"Oh, here's a photo of Frank riding up Roan Mountain." "Here are my friends,*

Dave and Karl." *"Oh, these must be the photos that Brenda took,"* he said as he thumbed through about five pictures of the birds. And then...the scream! *"Aaahhhh, Oh, my God, Calvin, who's asses are those?!!"* *"What kind of crazy things do you guys do on these trips?"* For perhaps the first time in his life, Calvin was speechless, and then he remembered. *"Momma, I loaned my camera to Brenda to take some photos. I had no idea she'd do something like this!"*

Unidentified Seyboros, behaving badly!

Of course, on our next ride, Calvin had a lot to say about his photographs. We let him talk, and to a person, we blamed Brenda. She tried to talk her way out of it, but the evidence was pretty clear. Calvin might just be finding out the real truth when he reads this book, and Brenda, you are hereby exonerated!

The Craziness of Bicycle Inn

Lots of crazy things happened at the Bicycle Inn. On one of our regular trips, Susan Hawkins crashed her bike on some railroad tracks and severely bruised her knee. She was with a few other riders. They sat there on the side of the tracks waiting for somebody to go get a vehicle to take her back to the Inn. While they were waiting, they heard a train whistle, and a moment later, a long train came slowly through the intersection.

As the engineer passed, he waved and threw what Susan thought was a bag of garbage at them. Up came her middle fingers, and lots of ugly words came flying out of her mouth! *"How dare you throw garbage at us, you ********!"* The train was going slowly enough that the engineer surely heard every word. A moment later, one of the other cyclists went to retrieve the 'trash' bag, only to find out it was a six-pack of ice-cold water! Oops, too late for Susan to recant! But the fun wasn't over yet.

The SAG vehicle finally arrived, and they loaded Susan into the back. They drove to the nearest store to get some ice, but the store did not sell it. What convenience store doesn't sell ice? Susan's knee was swelling badly, so somebody got the idea to buy a package of frozen sausage biscuits. They did the job, and we now had tomorrow's breakfast.

After that, Ernie Marshall came riding up to the store. Ernie was one of our club members, and he was a cancer doctor by profession. We were glad to see Ernie as we were worried about Susan's knee, and he was, after all, a doctor. He approached the rear of the vehicle, where we were all gathered. We explained that Susan had injured her knee. Ernie thought for a moment, then said, *"Ok, Susan. I'm gonna have to do a thorough exam. Remove your top and your shorts."* All of us burst out in laughter, including Susan, who was in a lot of pain, mind you!

The Periodic Knee Pain

Every trip to the Bicycle Inn was filled with fun, laughter, and camaraderie. I could go on forever, but I will close this chapter with the story about Karl Gerschutz's knee pain. We were gathered on the porch one day, talking a lot about nothing, which we were really good at. Somewhere in the conversation, Karl got to talking about an intermittent pain he would get in one of his knees. It was sporadic, it came and went for no obvious reasons.

After hearing about his pain, somebody said, *"Hey, ask Andy, he's a doctor."* Somebody else replied, *"Yeah, but he's an ENT (Ear, Nose, and Throat) doctor."* *"That might not matter,"* somebody else said. Andy was involved in a separate conversation at the time, so Karl waited until he was through and said, *"Hey, Andy, I am having these pains in my knee."* Karl explained the symptoms and then asked, *"Do you have any idea what could be causing the pain?"* Andy thought for a moment and then asked, *"When's the last time you had your prostate checked?"*

The whole group burst out in laughter, whereas Andy did not find it funny and got mad at us! Was he serious? What could the prostate have to do with knee pain? He started yelling that we weren't doctors, we wouldn't know. To this day, we joke about this. Whenever somebody mentions an ache or pain, somebody else may ask, *"Have you had your prostate checked?"* Before the weekend was over, somebody bought a jar of Vaseline and a rubber glove and presented them to Andy. He took it in good spirits and laughed along with the rest of us.

A few years ago, Mike and Pauline separated, and Mike moved away. The last we heard, the Bicycle Inn had been changed over to a Bed and Breakfast with maybe a French motif, we do not really know for sure. It was a sad ending for the entire bicycling community. However, the Seyboro Cyclists left their mark on those mountain roads around Bakersville. Similarly, Bicycle Inn certainly left its mark on our lives.

A Seyboro Memory

Many of our cycling rides took us to faraway places that required we stay in hotels overnight, sometimes for several nights. None of us were incredibly wealthy, so we always shared the hotel rooms, even 3 or 4 to a room at times, depending on room availability. Being the "elite" cyclists as we saw ourselves, we went to great lengths to pass ourselves off as 100% manly and macho (even though we were dressed in tight lycra from head to toe and sported shaved legs). We hoped strangers never noticed or questioned it, but, in fact, we shared rooms and sometimes, out of necessity, a bed. Steve 21 worked in the bike shop, Bicycle World, full-time. I worked part-time, perhaps 15 to 20 hours a week. One day

I was not working, and one of my motorcycling friends, Ken Arnold, went into the shop. Ken had gone into the shop looking for a pair of cycling shorts to wear under his jeans on his long-distance Harley rides.

Steve approached Ken and asked if he could help him. Ken looked at Steve and asked, "Hey, do you know Dave Galloway?" Steve, without missing a beat, replied, "Know him? Heck, I've slept with him!"

It didn't take long for the rumor to spread. My manly reputation was tarnished from that day forward!

Chapter 10
More Seyboro Rides

"There's a mean dog up ahead on the right. I don't need to be faster than the dog; I just need to be faster than you!"

-Jörg Wagner

Over many years, the Seyboro Cyclists have enjoyed thousands of rides together. Every ride was memorable in its own way and had moments where we have had our stomachs hurt with laughter. Cycling has always been our favorite entertainment, and *when in doubt, pedal it out* has always been our motto. I can only hope that I am correctly remembering and doing justice to many of the unique and fun events.

For over thirty years now, our club had advertised evening rides on Monday through Thursday, and daytime rides on Saturday and Sunday. Tuesday nights are reserved for new riders. We advertise a pace that will match their abilities. However, Wednesday nights have always been the 'Hammerfest,' where riders show up at their own peril.

The rest of the rides are ridden at a pace agreed upon by the folks who showed up for the ride. I am exceptionally proud that our club has survived without any formal leadership or officials over so many years. We have had a few rough times, with attendance falling to lowest numbers, but then things picked up again, and we would have 25 people show up for a Saturday ride.

Falling and getting back up

It is a part of life, no matter what profession or background. So, how can I say our rides were perfect? They were not! These rides were not always all about fun; we have had our fair share of crashes. But they are frequent in cycling because when you fly in the air, you have to be prepared for any kind of incident. What's important is how you always get back up after falling! It happens when you are riding inches apart from one another.

Several reasons cause crashes. The biggest cause is dogs crossing your path all of a sudden. There is something about a fast-moving bicycle that seems to bring out the primal instinct in some dogs. They are automatically attracted to speed. Get a large pit bull or another dog in the middle of 15 cyclists riding at 20mph, and it will wreak havoc among the group. Steve 21, Teresa Gerschutz, Velvie Hand, Agat McAllister, and I have all been hospitalized due to a dog attack. There have been many more. I wish I could remember all the names of cyclists who were severely injured due to the very reason.

In my case, I was taken down by a Great Dane near Snow Hill. This dog was huge, nearly as big as me, and he hit me broadside. We both went down. He got up before me and was getting ready to eat some flesh when the owner came running out of their house and got hold of him. Thank God, we wear helmets. It's a requirement in our club, and in the many injuries caused by the dogs, none have been head injuries.

I would like to take a second here to plead with dog owners. Restrain your dogs if you live anywhere near a road or highway. It's hard to blame the dog, they just do what dogs are supposed to do. It is your responsibility as the owner to take care of its whereabouts and make sure it does not hurt anyone. These dogs do not just hurt the cyclists, but often lose their own lives in the chaos. I can name five or more instances where a dog on the left side of the road saw us coming, launched into attack mode, and then got struck and killed by an oncoming car, as the dog came across the road to get to us. So please, restrain your dogs for both theirs and our safety, and spread the word to your friends.

We went through a stretch of crashes almost weekly, but it was due to our own stupid fault. I have mentioned earlier that every ride ends with a sprint for the finish. Most of our crashes occur on New Hope road within two hundred yards of the finish. We crazy cyclists are battling it out in a sprint for the finish, two or more get tangled up, and boom! Down goes everybody!

You would think we'd learn, but we don't! It's a mixture of adrenalin, testosterone, stubbornness, and, yes, stupidity! We will pick ourselves up, brush ourselves off, patch up our road rash, and do it all over again in a few days.

Over the years, we have seen hundreds of cyclists come and go. With the Air Force Base, we picked up new riders all the time, but they ended up moving to a different base in a few years. However, new members would show up, and it continued to evolve.

Other non-military folks come and go too, though many members have been with the club for about 15, 20, to even 25 years. Out of the group that showed up at the Herman Park Center many years ago when our club was formed, Rick Sessions and I continue to ride. I still see Randall Rigsby out by himself occasionally. Frank Drohan is still a good friend to all of us, but his health prevents him from riding, although I am adamant about bringing him back on the bike again one day!

Diesel Dave

During one of our club rides, I was given a nickname of 'Diesel Dave.' We were on a flat piece of road, and I was up at the front, pulling the group along at speeds more than 20 mph for several miles. Karl Gerschutz commented, *"Man, Dave is like a diesel locomotive up there!"* From that day onward, this name has stuck with me.

You have heard me talk about 'Steve 21' Desrochers; and he picked up this nickname much in the same manner. It seemed that every time Steve got up to the front, he would pull us along at about 21 mph, so he eventually became 'Steve 21.' We often joke with him in recent years as he's aged, should we start calling him 'Steve 13'?

Six Hills Road

Some of our favorite rides include 'Six Hills Road' near Grantham. The real name is Overman Road, but to us, it has always been 'Six Hills Road.' It's about two miles long and has anywhere from four to eight hills on it, depending on how we describe a hill. If the road goes up, straightens out, then goes up some more, is that one hill or two? We have never really settled that argument. Consequently, we call it 'Six Hills.' Whenever we go in that direction, as soon as we hit Six Hills Road, it's a wild race to the end, with bragging rights going to the first finisher until the next time.

Six Hills Road, July 4, 2006, Diesel Dave, Scott Summers, and Mike Haney

The Bartlett Road

We loved trying new routes. Hence, every now and then, one of us would discover a new place to ride, and we would all be ready to give it a try. Bartlett Road is yet another of our favorites, but nobody really knows where it is. This started years ago when Chuck Hand would be leading a ride, and no matter where we were, if we asked Chuck, he would say, *"Ahhh, I think we are on Bartlett Road."* Some of us figured he was only making that up. Three of our members tried to find Bartlett Road on Google Maps, and each of their computers crashed! Now, whenever we are out in the country, and we get lost, we assume we are on Bartlett Road.

The Death March

The Kenansville route has become known as the death march. When we rode it the first time, Frank Drohan suggested we ride to Kenansville and back on a Saturday. *"How far is it?"* We asked since none of us had ever been to Kenansville. *"It's about 30 miles,"* Frank told us. *"One way or round trip?"* We asked. *"Ahh... round trip,"* Frank replied. We should have known better because Frank rarely knew where he was or where he was going.

Anyway, we headed out for Kenansville on a Saturday morning. However, when our computers turned over to 30 miles, and we hadn't yet reached Kenansville, we knew we had been fooled by Frank again. The route was tough, with a lot of short, steep hills on it. We hit Kenansville at 35 miles, tired, thirsty, and out of water.

After stopping at a Hardees for water, we were on our way back home. *"I know a different route home,"* Frank told us. By now, you'd think we would know better than to listen to Frank, but we didn't! He was leading the ride, so we had to listen to him.

As we were approaching Mount Olive on our way back home, Frank announced, *"Just a mile or two up ahead is a cold-water spring with the freshest water you've ever tasted! Go ahead and empty your bottles."* Like a bunch of fools, each one of us did that except for Frank.

He finally pulled off the side of the road and pointed to an old lead pipe sticking up out of the ground with green water flowing out of it. *"Oh my God,"* we said. *"Check it out, it's cold,"* Frank told us. We each took a sip. It was cold, but it had so much iron in it, we got that feeling in our throats that you get with a bloody nose. *"We can't drink that,"* we told Frank.

By now, we were ready to kill him! However, he was the fastest rider among us at the time, and he still had water. We knew we could never catch him to kill him. Lucky for us, we came upon a store a few miles later and were able to get some potable water. We finished the day with about 75 miles, and the 'Kenansville Death March' became one of our regular routes.

These are just a few of the many roads we have ridden many, many times over the years!

The Seyboro Cyclists ride towards the Simply Natural Creamery near Hookerton, NC, on their memorial ride for Joe Austin, July, 2019.

Ralph, Judy, and our club rides!

I would really be missing out if I didn't mention Ralph and Judy Jodice in this chapter about our club rides. Ralph was a Major in the Air Force, an F-15 fighter pilot. They were stationed at Seymour Johnson on several occasions. They often showed up on a tandem bike, but sometimes rode individually.

The first time we met them, they showed up for a ride and surprised us when they popped open the back of their vehicle at the end of the ride and had cans of Yoo-hoo chocolate drink on ice. They immediately became our best friends! Ralph and Judy were a truly unique couple. Always friendly and cheerful and wanting to help keep the club running well. I believe it was Ralph, along with Karl Gerschutz and Greg 'Guido' Hawkes, who got together and designed our club jerseys. It continues to appear in bike rides across North Carolina.

Seyboro Cyclist Jersey

Ralph and Judy moved away several times. Each time they came back, Ralph had been promoted to a higher rank. When they left for the last time, he was on his way to serve in a high-ranking position in a foreign country. But he and Judy never forgot their Seyboro friends.

On several occasions, they invited some of us to Ralph's promotion ceremonies in Washington, D.C. We would arrive in D.C. to be wined and dined and treated like celebrities while we were there. We sat with some members of the Joint Chiefs of Staff to see Ralph promoted to Major General (2 stars) and Lieutenant General (3 stars). Through all of the pomp and circumstance, they always remained, just Ralph and Judy for us; friends and fellow cyclists. Some high-ranking military folks have a hard time putting their rank aside when they are not working, but it was never an issue with Ralph.

They Both are Real Gems

I remember a time back in 2008 or 2009. I was scheduled to undergo a 6-hour surgery for my abdomen to repair some damage resulting from a bike accident back in 2006. Ralph and Judy made a special trip to Goldsboro to participate in a bike ride the club held in my honor, just before I went under the knife.

This truly humbled me. During the ride, on our way to New Bern, NC, Ralph had a flat tire. We stopped to fix it. Several of us tried to wrestle the wheel from Ralph to do the job for him. After all, he was a 2-star general. He shouldn't have to fix his flat. But he persisted, and Jörg ended up taking a picture of General Ralph, sitting on the side of the road, repairing his flat tire. That's the kind of man he is.

In 2013, when Ralph was retiring from the Air Force, our friend Karl Gerschutz was killed in a bike crash in Arizona. Despite the hecticness of retiring and trying to move and settle into their retirement home, Ralph and Judy took the time, along with Frank and I, as we made the long drive to Ohio to attend Karl's funeral. That's the kind of friends they are!

They are now living out their retirement years in Pennsylvania, but we keep in touch, and they look us up when they are in town. Ralph and Judy, thanks for all you did for the Seyboro Cyclists!

The Bike VA

A group of Seyboros also participated in some Bike Virginia events over the years. Bike VA is an organized 5-day bike ride around different areas of Virginia. They usually have about 2,000 cyclists in attendance. Each day, they offer several mileage options. Tom Bradshaw was a big fan of the event, and he invited a few of us to attend one of the rides in 2003.

Bobby Baker finds a version of 'Looka Hill' in Virginia.

It was a blast, very well planned and organized. Mike Haney and I did that ride with Tom in 2003, and we were hooked. We ended up doing five or six of these rides together, and we always met up with Tom's brother, Richard, and his wife, Lynn. Those rides created many fond memories. Some other Seyboros who participated in the ride at one time or another included Bobby and Karen Baker, Lisa Mathias, Karl Gerschutz, Frank Drohan, and Mike Haney's wife, Helen.

2009 Bike Virginia, Diesel Dave, Tom Bradshaw, and Mike Haney.

Rest assured, any time there were two or more Seyboro Cyclists together, laughter and good times were guaranteed!

A Seyboro Memory

On one of our club century rides to the beach, Mike Haney announced he was taking his tandem bike, and he offered all the ladies in the club the opportunity to ride with him at 20-mile intervals. The rest of us males were all a little jealous of Mike; we're on a bike by ourselves while Mike took turns riding with all the cute ladies. Naturally, Mike took a lot of ribbing about this, but he never stopped smiling. About 50 miles into the trip, Mike had Carissa on the back of his bike. We were riding along at a good clip, and somebody announced, "riders off", meaning somebody had dropped off the back and was unable to hold our pace. We slowed down and I realized it was the tandem that had fallen off. They caught back up and we picked up the pace a little, and sure enough they fell off again. This happened 3 or 4 times. It was unusual because Mike and Carissa were both strong riders. Finally, the 5th time this happened, the group pulled off to the side of the road to wait. When they caught back up, they stopped and Carissa dismounted the back of the bike. She was crying. Somebody asked, "What's wrong, Carissa?" She sobbed a few more times, then replied, "I'm...I'm...I'm...pregnant." Complete silence enveloped the group for about 5 seconds until Bobby Baker hollered, "Da** you, Haney!" Everyone erupted in laughter including Carissa.

In reality Carissa was in the early stages of her pregnancy. She and her husband, Paige, had not wanted to make it public yet. But riding the bike at a fairly fast clip was having an effect on her in her condition. Over the years, we've never let Mike forget about this, and we often warn our new lady riders, "Don't ride the tandem with Haney unless you want to get pregnant!"

Chapter 11
Seyboros Gone Racing

Tour de Moore

Although Seyboros spent a significant chunk of their lives cycling, the club's early racing exposure was the most prominent at the Tour de Moore near Southern Pines, NC. It was an annual professional race, but they offered races for amateur riders with visions of stardom. We usually took a large group to participate, and we routinely represented ourselves well.

I remember during one of our races, a Sheriff's deputy stopped us halfway through it. He was a 'Barney Fife' type of character. We were rolling along at almost 30 mph when he came racing past our peloton and pulled his car sideways across the road, forcing us to stop. He jumped out of the car with his whistleblowing and hands in the air, indicating that we should stop.

There were nearly a hundred cyclists in the race. We all came to a stop. 'Barney' was screaming, *"What do y'all think you're doing out here racing on my roads?"*

Somebody tried to explain that we were involved in a U.S. Cycling Federation amateur bike race. The officials had obtained all the permissions and approvals. Several others told him they weren't 'his' roads! This did not appease Barney. He said we were going to wait right there while he called his boss. He was going to drag everyone into his jail if necessary.

While he was engaged in his call, Frank said to me, *"Hey Dave, follow me."* Frank went around the side of the group on the grassy area, past Officer Barney and his car, and off we went. Barney saw us at the last minute and started yelling and blowing his whistle, but we were gone. Barney now had to make a choice. Chase after Frank and me, or keep the other large group of cyclists stopped. He opted to keep the large group stopped until he spoke with his boss. Frank and I were on our breakaway. Perhaps we would win this race!

We hammered as fast as we could, but the main group caught up with us in about 15 minutes. Barney had finally released them and put his bullet back in his pocket. Of course, the cyclists were none too happy with Frank and me, but Frank was always known to believe in, *"All is fair in love, war, and bike racing!"* Anyway, we both got swallowed up in the finishing sprint, and neither of us won.

June 1989 – AT&T Corporate Cycling Challenge

Another exciting race was the AT&T Corporate Cycling Challenge in Princeton, New Jersey. This was a team time trial race, open to any group of four cyclists belonging to a company or business across the United States. I found out about the race and convinced Seymour Johnson Air Force Base to allow four of us to enter the race.

Richard Synger at Quality Bike Shop paid the entry fee, and Frank Drohan's copier company assisted with our expenses. Our team was made up of four active-duty enlisted members: my friends Dave Scarano, Tim Scott, Mike Luke, and me. All four of us were strong riders and evenly matched in our cycling skills.

We would need to ride as hard and as fast as we could, depending on each other to take very short pulls at the front, then dropping to the back, catching our breath a little, as the other three riders took short turns at the front. As I mentioned earlier, it takes considerably more effort to be at the front because of the wind. The ones following save a little bit of energy by drafting. A good team can be poetry in motion as they work together. It's a beautiful sight to witness. The four of us spent a month training and practicing, and we felt we were up for the challenge. We departed Seymour Johnson for Princeton, NJ, and hoped to make our base proud of us. We were wearing Air Force jerseys, but we were all Seyboro Cyclists as well.

The Day of the Challenge

We arrived to quite a party atmosphere. There were about 900 participants ready to roll their bicycles. We checked in and got our starting time and location. They told us that we would be riding a 13.5-mile team time trial, just like all the others. It was a rectangular route, and we would ride it four times. The team who finished the route in the fastest time possible would be the winner. They had categories established for different types of businesses. We were in the "Government" category. We were confident we could win our category, but we were also looking for the overall win. Why not aim high, like the Air Force Motto? Teams were starting out at 1-minute intervals. When our time finally came, the four of us lined up side by side, with people holding each of us up. We were clipped onto our pedals and ready to ride. When the horn sounded, we were off.

We quickly stretched out into a 4-man formation, with each of us taking short pulls at the front, then dropping to the back of the line. One negative issue was immediately apparent: the strong wind gusts! Riding into a tough headwind will sap your strength quickly. On a rectangular route, you will eventually have a tailwind, but I don't think the tailwind ever makes up for the headwind's extra work.

Nevertheless, we hammered as fast as we could, and we actually passed nine of the teams that had started out before us. We continued our rotation process for the next 32 minutes and 15 seconds when we crossed the finish line for the 4th and final time. We were elated! The results so far showed that our average speed was just a tad over 25mph, so we knew we had done well. But was it good enough to win the day?

Before our race, we had been checking out our competition. The biggest threat we suspected was from a team of four men from the Pentagon. We had chatted with them. They were all a little younger than us, and they talked like they had ridden some pretty fast time trials. They were starting three minutes behind us, so we'd certainly be looking for them after we finished. The race officials told us we had one of the fastest times of the day. All we could do now was wait. We were still breathing heavily from our efforts, but we gathered near the finish line to see how our foes from the Pentagon would finish. We waited… and waited… and never saw them come across the finish line. Had something happened? A flat tire or other malfunction would be devastating in such a short race. Perhaps, they'd dropped out. All we could do now was wait until the closing ceremony, several hours away.

The Final Ceremony

When we all gathered for the final ceremony, we were happy to hear that we had finished fourth overall out of 220 teams who participated. We were ecstatic! Now, imagine our surprise when they announced the number one overall finisher. You have probably guessed it already; yes, it was the team from the Pentagon. We were a little bit baffled, as we had never seen them finish. We were happy that we had finished 4th overall and 2nd in our category. Not a bad days' work! We accepted our second-place trophy with a lot of pride and dignity. After a good meal with a lot of calories, we were on the road back home to North Carolina.

"Dave Scarano, Diesel Dave, Mike Luke, Tim Scott"

Had we been bushwhacked?

But wait... before leaving, the management had furnished everybody with the recorded times for all the teams and categories. We were on the New Jersey Turnpike, and Mike Luke was studying the list. He noticed the Pentagon team was listed for having ridden their time trial in 25 minutes, 11 seconds, at a whopping 32mph! It is quite unbelievable because there are professional teams who cannot do that. Had we been bushwhacked?

There are several things wrong with this picture. First, as I just mentioned, was their average speed. Secondly, if they started three minutes after us and finished the race in 25:11, they would have caught us and passed us on the course. They did not do that. Nobody passed us, and if we never saw them finish after we did, it left us with just one explanation; they only rode three laps, not four. That's the only scenario that makes any sense.

They would have averaged a respectable 24mph for 3 laps, but still weren't as fast as us. The lap counters were some college kids who were supposed to be keeping track of each team and how many laps they had ridden. However, they were spending a lot of time talking and joking as they worked. It would have been easy to make a mistake. The only ones who would have known differently were the Pentagon guys, and hey, who can blame them if they rode three laps and were told they were done? They walked away with two first-place trophies!

We will never know for sure. But either way, we felt we represented the Air Force and the Seyboro Cyclists well in New Jersey.

June 1991 – The Race of The Truth!

Time-trialing was always my strong suit in cycling. Two of my proudest moments were the times I won bronze medals, the third place, in the North Carolina amateur cycling time-trials. This race was open to anyone who held an amateur's bicycle racing license issued by the United States Cycling Federation. A group of us traveled to Wilmington, NC, to compete. We all held licenses and competed in our age groups. I was competing in the age group of 35-40 years. My close friends Frank Drohan and Dave Scarano attended, along with Brian Brothers and a few other Seyboros.

A time trial is also called 'The race of truth.' Riders start out at intervals, normally a minute apart, and ride a specific distance all by themselves; no drafting is allowed. The state time-trials were 40 kilometers or 24.85 miles. A big goal among cyclists is to ride a 40k time-trial in less than one hour. We all aspired to do this, but more than that, we just hoped to win or place in our individual age group.

It was an out and back course with a few small hills. To our surprise and delight, Frank, Dave, and I all finished slightly under one hour. I think Frank and I both rode about a 59:45 race, and Dave finished in 59:58. I remember that well because he nearly ran into a table and some spectators as he pedaled furiously to beat the clock, and nearly lost control of his bike at the very end.

We were all so happy to have finished under an hour as we climbed into Frank's car and headed home. All three of us had reached a cycling pinnacle by riding 40 kilometers in less than an hour. The essential thing to note here is that we were all riding 'regular' road bikes. Times have changed in the past 30 years, and time-trial bikes and clothing have all become much more sophisticated since we made our marks.

Little did Frank and I know, but a year later, we attended the time trial races again. When the official saw us, he said, *"I've got something for you guys."* It turned out, both Frank and I had earned bronze medals in our age groups for our performances in 1991, but we had left before the awards ceremony. The race official had been carrying our medals around in his car for the whole past year.

In 1992, I rode even better than in the 1991 ride. I rode the course in 58 minutes and 8 seconds for an average speed of 25.6 mph. This time, I hung around for the ceremony and learned that I had again won the bronze medal. I was beaten by the same two guys both years, but I had nothing to be ashamed of. That was evidently the 'peak' of my career because I never rode that fast again. Age has a way of catching up with all of us sooner or later!

2002 – Hotter 'n Hell

Our friends, Ralph and Judy Jodice invited us to come to Wichita Falls, Texas in 2002, to compete in the Hotter 'n Hell Hundred bike ride. Ralph served as the Wing Commander there and offered to put us up for a few days. I am sure when they extended the invitation, they didn't expect six of us to accept.

So early on a Thursday morning, Frank, Karl, Bobbie Baker, Mike Haney, Tim Shockley, and I headed out on a 24-hour road trip. We were in Frank's suburban, pulling a trailer with a Seyboro Cyclists banner. We made the 1,200-mile trip non-stop and pulled up to Ralph and Judy's house at 6AM on Friday. I know they were saying, *"What were we thinking!"* But they were extremely gracious hosts.

After a short nap, we went for a bike ride, and then Ralph and Judy took us on a tour of the base. We started to settle down late in the afternoon, preparing for the big ride the next day. Temperatures were predicted to reach 107 degrees, but nothing ever had stopped us from riding.

As we prepared for the ride, I noticed Frank was using a new drink mix. He and I had ridden many miles together, and we had always used Gatorade for long distances. But this time, he was preparing a new drink. I said, *"Hey Frank, it's probably not a good idea to try a new drink on a big ride like this."* He said, *"Well, Paul Harrell told me I should use this stuff. He swears by it."*

Paul was a friend and fellow Seyboro. Frank and I had started working with him as a teenager, and he had turned into a really strong cyclist. I told Frank that I thought he was making a mistake. I even told him Paul might just be messing with him, but Frank would not hear it. Paul would not steer him wrong.

The Beginning

We were up at 5AM on a Saturday and headed to downtown, where we met up with eight thousand other cyclists. Can you imagine how long a starting line is with that many riders? At 7AM, they started the ride with a cannon shot, and the cannon happened to be located right next to where we were standing. What an explosion! We did not move for about 5 minutes, and then we started inching forward.

It probably took us 15 minutes before we could actually ride our bikes without fear of running into someone else. We had hoped to stay together, but then it all fell apart about 20 minutes into the ride. There were just too many cyclists. We each found a group riding at a pace we were comfortable with and settled in for 100 miles of hotter 'n hell! It was already in the high nineties, and the day was young.

At about 25 miles, my group caught up with Frank. He told me he was not feeling well, and his stomach looked like he had swallowed a basketball. I cautioned him to take it easy. My group hammered on at about 20 mph, leaving Frank in our wake, and the temperature kept rising.

At about 50 miles, I came across Mike Haney on the side of the road with a flat tire. I stopped to help him. Mike is one of my favorite cycling friends. He had used up all his spare inflators and still had a flat. I was able to get him back on the road. Mike tells me to this day that if I had not stopped to help him, he might still be sitting on the side of that road.

"*Diesel Dave and Bobby Baker, Hotter 'n Hell*"

At about 60 miles, we came across a huge SAG stop. There were hundreds of cyclists there, reloading drinks and cooling down in some water misting tents. Just about our entire team met up there, except for Karl. We knew he was upfront with the real hammerheads and had no plans to stop.

Somebody said they'd seen Frank, on his hands and knees in front of a VFW building 10 miles back, and he was vomiting. So much for Paul Harrell's magic energy drink! What was ironic, Frank is a Marine Corps veteran, a huge patriot, and fan of the U.S. Military; of all places to stop and vomit, he picked a VFW building! Ralph eventually found Frank sitting in one of the tents under the water, and Frank refused to leave. He said he was done! He was going to try and find the fastest and easiest way back to the finish line. He would meet us there.

The End

Leaving Frank behind, the rest of us headed out for the remaining 40 miles ride. We were able to stay together as a group for most of the remaining trip. The temperature reached a scorching high of 108 degrees as we crossed the finishing line in about 6 hours. Karl had finished about an hour before us. Frank came limping in a little bit later with the little old ladies and small children on their bikes. He has never heard the end of this to this day! I still think Paul Harrell gave Frank some bad information on his energy drink. There was a reason for this, and it dealt with our

Father's Day ride a few months before this ride. You will see my reasoning in the next chapter. All the pitfalls aside, we were all proud of our accomplishments, including Frank. Despite his problems, he had managed to ride about 80 miles in extreme temperatures. We attended a barbecue that afternoon hosted by another Seyboro who was now stationed at Shepard Air Force Base. At 6PM, we hugged Ralph and Judy, thanked them, and wished them goodbye and were on the road back home.

It was quite a road trip for us, just one of the many. We still tell stories about it, and we always will! The Seyboro Cyclists have had so many fun and entertaining rides, and I can only relate a few in these limited pages. Perhaps a sequel down the road would help...?

A Seyboro Memory

For many years I had a running battle with Chuck Hand to see which one of us would get the honor of the most cycling miles for the year. I went quite a few years with 6,000 to 7,000 miles on the bike, and Chuck was always quite close to me. We had a lot of fun bantering back and forth about which one of us would win the contest on

December 31.

Most of us cyclists keep mileage logs and are quite serious about logging our daily miles. I am not the only one who would finish up a ride with, let's say 57.7 miles, so I would ride a few loops around the block to make it an even 58 miles. When I entered 58 miles in my diary, I wanted it to be true.

Chuck was also good friends with Jörg, and Jörg spent some time over at Chuck's house. Chuck's wife, Velvie, made the mistake of telling Jörg where Chuck kept his mileage diary.

Jörg was well aware of the mileage challenge that was going on between Chuck and me. So, when he was at Chuck's house, he would take a peek at his mileage diary. He would then feed the information to me. *"Hey, Dave, as of today, Chuck has 4,685 miles."*

I made good use of this information. When Chuck and I showed up to ride the next day, he would invariably ask me, *"Hey, Dave, how many miles do you have for the year?"* I would look down at my bicycle computer, pretend to thumb through the functions, and reply, *"I just turned over 4,700 miles."* He would get a look on his face like, *"Man, how does he stay just ahead of me?"*

Even when he didn't ask, if Jörg had recently looked into his diary, I would wait until I was in the middle of a ride with Chuck and comment, "Wow, I just now went over 6,400 miles for the year!" Knowing full well that Chuck had ridden only a few miles less than that.

I had a lot of fun with this, but eventually, Chuck caught up with what I was up to. After that, I would ask Chuck, *"How many miles do you have this year?"* And his reply would always be, *"One more mile than you have!"*

Chapter 12
The Legacy Continues

What does the future hold for the Seyboro Cyclists? We have been around for 35 years now, or you can say for more than half of my life! Together, we have participated in the craziest of rides and won countless medals for our club. Ironically, I have aged out of participating in most of the rides. It is almost as if we never really cared about the time we spent in cycling, we simply lived through it all.

Cycling never made us feel we were growing old. We have several members in their seventies who continue to ride well; Mike Haney, Ron Gray, and Gerry Soud, to name a few. I still ride a bike, and I hope to continue until the day I die. However, the accident I was involved in 13 years ago, has taken its toll on my body. I am sure the club would welcome me warm-heartedly to ride with them again, but I would slow them down, and I never wish to do that.

The SloBros

My good friend Jörg has come up with an alternative,

though. It is sort of a sub-chapter of the Seyboro Cyclists. It's aptly named 'SloBros' and is geared to the folks like me who, for one reason or another, can no longer hold the typical pace of the main body of the club members.

A little history on our club jerseys may also be in order here. I mentioned in an earlier chapter earlier, our jerseys were designed by Ralph Jodice, Karl Gerschutz, and 'Guido' Hawkes. They came up with the initial design, and then other club members were asked to give input. We are exceptionally proud of the end results, especially the logo on our jersey. It shows an F-15 fighter plane and the words 'Follow Us.'

Seymour Johnson Air Force Base in Goldsboro is home to the 4th Fighter Wing and has three squadrons of F-15 Strike Eagles. The F-15s were used extensively in the First Gulf War and have been involved in our war on terrorism since the twin towers were destroyed in 2001. Goldsboro is very proud of the history and accomplishments of Seymour Johnson. Probably a good half of our club members over the years have been active duty and retired Air Force members and their families.

The part of our logo that says 'Follow Us' is a subtle message to other cyclists; follow us if you can keep up with our pace. Many of the rides we have done with lots of other clubs in attendance have witnessed the Seyboro jerseys at the very front, leading the pack. If somebody from another club dared to pass us, at least one of our members would leave them behind, and be on the front again. It was our way to put out the message that you have no choice but to follow us!

So, when Jörg came up with the SloBros, he had decals made. They said, 'Follow us. It's really easy!' This is a joke on ourselves, as we just don't ride that fast anymore. But the important part is, we are still riding!

On many days, folks will see Jörg and I out there plugging along. We are often accompanied by Lisa Mathias, Wendy Hicks, and George Howell, who, at the age of 84, still rides a bike better than many. Sometimes, others join us in the ride too. Just as with the Seyboros, anybody is welcomed to ride with the SloBros.

For a number of years, they called me 'The Prez,' though I don't remember ever being elected President. I stepped down from my 'presidency' a few years ago. I didn't feel right scheduling rides that I knew I would not be attending. Right away, Rick Sessions, Benny Hood, Joe Austin, and Chuck Millard jumped up to fill the void, but our group really doesn't need much of the usual leadership. Folks still manage to show up at the scheduled times and ride, have fun, make memories, and love one another. What more can you ask for?

Charitable and Civic Events

This book would surely be incomplete if I did not mention the many charitable and civic events we have performed. We have held a ride at the time of Christmas for more than 20 years now, to raise money for the Goldsboro Family Y's annual Christmas party for needy families. We have probably averaged $1,000 each year, only by passing a hat among our members before heading out for a cold, windy December bike ride.

We have come to the financial aid of others in times of

need. The club was a big part of my family's fund-raising effort when I had my accident in 2006. I will always remember their efforts; the emotional and financial participation in the matter. They raised thousands of dollars that made it possible for Kay and my children to make the daily 70-mile round trip drive to the hospital, paying for meals, gas, and parking fees. What would we have done without them?

When David Carter lost his job right after putting a new bike on layaway at Christmas time, a group of us pitched in and bought the bike for him. The look on his face when we gave him the bike was all the thanks we needed! Our club has also spent countless hours performing volunteer work, helping with traffic control during fund-raising events for the Family Y and other groups.

We spent five years with the 'Adopt a Highway' program, where we went and gathered trash along the New Hope Road several times a year. These were not just charity works but experiences of a lifetime. We learned from this particular cleaning project that if cigarettes, alcohol, and fast-food restaurants were eliminated, there would be no roadside trash!

The Synonymous Seyboros

Unfortunately, you won't find an attachment of our club membership. It's not due to a lack of effort! I have worked for several months to come up with a list, but it's like chasing an impossible dream. My current list is over 300 names, but I fear, despite my best efforts and the aid of several other long-time members, that I would inadvertently still miss a few important names. There are hundreds of members that I have not mentioned in any of these chapters, but each of them has been an important part of the Seyboros. And 35 years of members joining and leaving the club is a long time. So here's my offer; contact me after you've read this book and I will gladly share my list with you. Perhaps with time and my readers' help I could ensure an accurate list.

Nevertheless, I want to do justice to every person who has ever shown up for one of our rides. They have each been a part of something massive. We are a group of friends who shared some time with others on challenging rides. They helped get each other through a fierce headwind with words of encouragement or asking them to sit in behind and enjoy the pull. We tell folks to come out and ride with us for a couple of times, and they become members of the Seyboro

Cyclists forever. I can only hope that each one of them knows they have been a part of something special.

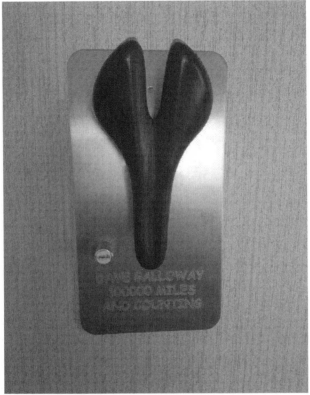

"Who would have thought, back in 1985, that 20 years later the club would be presenting me this plaque?!"

Another Father's Day Ride - 2002

I think it only fits that I end this book with another funny story. Not surprisingly, it was a Father's Day ride, just like the one described in Chapter one. This one was held in 2002, starting and ending in downtown La Grange. It is no wonder that it includes Frank Drohan again! These events stand out in my head as if it was yesterday.

We were riding a metric century again. There was a large crowd just like the previous one, and several of us 'hammerheads' were ready to battle it out from beginning to end. It was a warm Saturday, and we started out at 9 AM. The route was one of North Carolina's famous cycling routes, called Bike Route 40, and it was well marked with signs.

The 5-man breakaway or 3?

There were five of us in a breakaway within the first 15 minutes of the ride, including myself, Frank, Karl, Paul Harrell, and Teddy Young. Four of us were from Goldsboro. However, Teddy was from Kinston. We were all Seyboros, but a rumor circulated that Teddy was going for the win and was being sponsored by the bike shop in Kinston. The rest of us were all sponsored by Bicycle World in Goldsboro, and it had always been a big supporter of the Seyboro Cyclists.

I had spoken with Frank and Karl before the ride, and we

had decided that we would make every effort to bring home the win for Bicycle World. Our little 5-man breakaway was hammering, determined not to let anybody catch us. About 10 miles into the ride, Teddy announced he had to stop and pee. *"Are you guys gonna stop with me?"* asked Teddy. *"Sure, we will,"* one of us replied. Teddy pulled off the side of the road, and Paul Harrell pulled over with him. Frank, Karl, and I put the hammer down and kept going! *"Sorry, Teddy and Paul."* As I said earlier, all is fair in love, war, and cycling! They hollered obscenities as we rode away.

For the next 40 miles or more, we could see Paul and Teddy back there chasing us. They remained between ¼ and ½ mile behind us. Frank, Karl, and I put ourselves into time trial mode, taking short pulls at the front of our group, then dropping back to catch our breath. Paul and Teddy were doing the same thing. We had a slight advantage on them, three men against 2. We were all very evenly matched when it came to cycling skills.

At one point, my group got held up, waiting to cross a busy highway. In that time, Paul and Teddy got within a hundred yards of catching us. But we were determined, worked harder, and slowly opened up the gap again.

At another point, we made a right turn, a particularly sharp turn, sharper than 90 degrees. So, as we were riding, we could see Paul and Teddy approaching the turn we had just made. Paul was hollering, *"Hey guys, wait on us!"* *"Sure!"* We answered as we continued to pedal as fast as we could.

At last, we won for the Bicycle World!

Somewhere around 50 miles, we lost Paul and Teddy. We could no longer see them behind us, even on the long, straight stretches. Getting out of your opponents' sight can have a demoralizing effect on them. We didn't let up, though, and crossed the finish line at 2:45. Karl nipped Frank and me in the final sprint. There were a lot of clubs and family members at the finish line to cheer for us, including Frank's sister, Charlotte, who was in town from Iowa visiting Frank.

Afterward, we waited at the finish line for Paul, Teddy, and all the others to finish. Frank was telling Charlotte, *"Paul Harrell is one of my very best friends! I hope he isn't too mad at us."* After about a ten-minute wait, we saw a lone rider coming toward us. As he got closer, we realized it was

Paul. We all began yelling and cheering for him. But as he crossed the finishing line, he looked at us, raised both middle fingers in the air, and began a long stream of cuss words. He never stopped. Instead, he rode straight to where his car was parked, threw his bike in the back of his SUV, got in the car, and started the engine. He burned rubber while again flashing us the middle finger as he drove away.

Charlotte looked at Frank and asked, *"Gee Frank, do all of your really good friends treat you that way?"*

Well, we figured Paul might be a little upset with us when we rode away and did not wait for him and Teddy. But we thought our number one priority was to make sure one of the Bicycle World riders finished first. Obviously, Paul felt we had done him wrong. He was upset that we did not stop with him and Teddy earlier in the ride. He stayed angry with us for a month or so, and then we were friends again.

Revenge maybe?

Several months after this incident, we were preparing to leave for the Hotter 'n Hell Hundred in Texas. Paul introduced Frank to a new energy drink and suggested Frank try it during the ride. This is the drink I talked about in the last chapter that got Frank's stomach upset to the point he could not finish the ride. I asked Paul about this when we returned from Texas. His reply was, *"Now Dave, would I do something like that?"* I am willing to bet he would. However, Frank does not think so. I guess we will never know for sure!

The book may end, but Seyboros continue to roll!

I know I can write a thousand pages and still not be satisfied with the experiences I put out there for the readers. But for now, my book comes to an end. However, Seyboro Cyclists continue to ride, creating even more fun memories.

We occasionally meet for a few beers or ride to the ice cream shop to indulge in some calories. Then get back on the bikes to burn the calories. It's a never-ending cycle, at least one we never want to end. The faces will change over time, but I hope I have done a good job of memorializing our history. Each Seyboro is truly special and unique in their own way, and together, we have made a lot of history.

It's a bittersweet feeling, bringing this book to an end. There are so many stories that are left untold, stories about a ragtag group of people who came together many years ago. They have had such a tremendous impact on my life and, I hope, each other's lives too. When I look over my past life, the Seyboro Cyclists bicycle club is among the top-most things that has affirmatively affected my life.

I hope you love the lightheartedness of this book and will continue to follow my story in my next sequel, 'Chasing Seyboro.' Yes, even my next book includes our club because the bike club played a huge part in my life immediately following my accident, and for the many years since it happened. They have always been there for me, and it would not be wrong to say that they all have become a part of who I am today. What a fantastic group of people!

Glossary of Cycling Terms

(Seyboro comments in *italics*)

Break or Breakaway: One or more cyclists take off from the front of a group. *The only time Dave has ever been truly truly pi**ed off.*

Century: Normally refers to a 100-mile ride. A metric century is 100 kilometers, or about 62 miles. *Both are must-do-milestones for every cyclist.*

Dog up: A warning to the group that a dog is up ahead and getting ready to attack the group. *I don't have to be faster than the dog. I just need to be faster than you!*

Double century: This is a true test of endurance and skill. Two hundred miles, normally ridden in 10 to 16 hours, is a demanding task even for pro cyclists. *Historically about 25% of the starters make it. Others succumb to fatigue. One member met his fate outside of a gas station in La Grange, NC.*

Draft or Drafting: Following the other rider(s) close enough to reduce the effects of the wind. *Other than cornering, something else tri-geeks are terrible at.*

Drop: The results of a successful breakaway. A rider or riders can't hold the speed of the pack, and they fall off the back of the group. *What happens to sprinters on an overpass!*

Echelon: A formation used by cyclists to combat the winds coming from an oblique angle, e.g., With a strong wind coming from my right front side, I'll position myself slightly beside and behind the left side of rider in front of me. This formation can cause cyclists to take up an entire lane of the road. *What drivers hate.*

Gap: The distance between one or more cyclists and the ones who are chasing them. *What you're trying to create when you can't win a sprint to save your life.*

Gearing: You will often hear cyclists say, "I needed my 39-28 to get up that hill," or "We were going so fast I had to go to my 53-12." Here they are talking about the number of teeth on their front and rear sprockets. The closer your front sprocket matches your rear sprocket, the easier it becomes to pedal the bike, but you won't be going very fast, normally used going uphill. When your front sprocket is considerably larger than the rear, you will need to pedal harder but will travel much faster. *What some 'real' cyclists don't use in the* winter; they insist on riding a single speed bike to make them stronger.

Hammer: Riding as hard as one can. *Or really, just faster than the guy you're with.*

Hammerhead: A strong cyclist. *One who always proves he's faster than you.*

Hold my wheel: The lead rider cuts through the wind. The following cyclist stays as close as possible to the rear wheel of the leader. It's estimated that the one in back works about 25% less than the one in front. *The last words heard before Karl pulled 4 guys into a 15-mph headwind for 83 miles.*

Motor-pacing: Following a motorized vehicle to take advantage of drafting. *When you just **have** to get 3 bottles back to the pack on the Pickle Ride, or, **Cheating** in the words of Steve 21.*

Paceline: Riders rotate positions in a line, each one taking a turn at the front where he or she pulls into the wind before swinging off. *By far the most important skill on Four Way Rd.*

Pack or Peloton: A group of cyclists riding together. *What we are versus what we think we look like.*

Pull: Term for a rider who sits at the front of the pack and cuts through the wind, making it easier for the ones behind, e.g., take a pull. *A rider who sits up front for as long as they can, riding to a point of near exhaustion, trying to show the rest of us how strong they are ... and then gets blown out on the way back from Kenansville. Every. Single. Time.*

SAG Stop: A stationary stop positioned along the route with drinks, food and repair equipment. *A place where no self-respecting cyclist would ever be seen stopping.*

SAG Vehicle: A vehicle that travels the route with drink, food and repair equipment. Also has a few seats for those who have to drop out of the ride. *A place of shame for a self-proclaimed real cyclist. They sit in the back with their head hung low, hoping nobody sees them.*

Sit-in: A rider who rides in the peloton but does not take any pulls at the front. *OK, Seyboros, you know who you are!*

Tandem: A bicycle built for two. *Why would anybody want their spouse with them on a bike ride?*

Tri-geek: A cyclist's nickname for a triathlete. There is some friendly banter that goes on between the pure cyclists, and the triathletes who participate in cycling, swimming, and running. Some cyclists feel the "tri-geeks" lack many of the necessary bicycling skills to ride in a group. *Tri-geeks* *disagree with this assessment, as they crash going into the next turn.*

USCF: Back in the 80s and 90s, this was the national governing body for bike racing in the United States. Sometime over the years the name became USA Cycling.

Wheel Sucker: A cyclist who sits behind the others and won't take a turn at the front of the pack. *Again, Seyboros, you know who you are!*

A Look Forward

My next book will tell the remarkable story of my bicycle crash in 2006, resulting in hospitalization for months, countless therapies, multiple surgeries, and recovery. I continue to experience problems today, more than 13 years later. To know more about what really happened, hang on for my next sequel.

As I bring this book to a close, I want to present a picture of something the Seyboro Cyclists did for me while I was hospitalized. In February of 2007, while I was a patient at the Lifecare Hospital in Rocky Mount, NC, the club arranged a ride of nearly 60 miles to visit me. These true friends rode in near freezing temperatures, fighting a cold headwind out of the north for the entire ride, to pay me a visit in the hospital. I believe the photo says it all! I love you, Seyboros!

BEING SEYBORO

Made in the USA
Columbia, SC
23 May 2021